Where There's **Change** There's **Opportunity!**

Success strategies for enhancing your health, wealth and happiness!

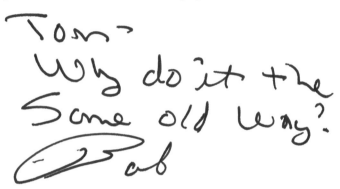

Compiled by **Doug Smart**

James & Brookfield

J&B

Publishers

Where There's Change There's Opportunity!

Cover Design:	PAULA CHANCE
Editing:	GELIA DOLCIMASCOLO
Proof Reader:	LAURA JOHNSON
Book Layout:	DARLENE NICHOLAS

For more information, contact:
James & Brookfield Publishers
P.O. Box 768024
Roswell, GA 30076
(770) 587-9784

Library of Congress Catalog Number 98-67155

ISBN: 0-9658893-5-1

10 9 8 7 6 5 4 3 2 1

Dedication

Dedicated to ever faster and more powerful computers.
Whether we love them, ignore them, or hate them, they have shifted our lives into hyper-drive.

Contents

*"There is nothing more difficult to carry out,
nor more doubtful of success, nor more
dangerous to handle than to initiate a new order
of things. For the reformer has enemies in all who
profit by the old order, and only lukewarm defenders
in those who would profit by the new order.
This lukewarmness arises partly from the
fear of their adversaries, who have the law in
their favour; and partly from the incredulity
of mankind, who do not truly believe in anything
new until they have actual experience of it."*

MACHIAVELI — The Prince (1513)

"It's easy to come up with new ideas; the hard part is letting go of what worked for you two years ago, but will soon be out-of-date."

ROGER VONOECH

"It's amazing what ordinary people can do if they set out without preconceived notions."

CHARLES F. KETTERING

"In a time of drastic change, it is the learner who will inherit the future."

ERIC HOFFER

"Look at the grandness. The big picture. Not what is wrong. Get out of the box."

WALT DISNEY

Introduction

In an essay about change in a recent issue of Life magazine, the writer wondered — if an educated person living at the end of the 19th Century forecast what life at the end of the 20th Century would be like, how close would he or she be? The writer surmised that compared to the Industrial Revolution, the inventions and conventions of the 20th Century were so wildly different, the future thinking person would have missed by light years. That got me to thinking — if you asked an educated person living at the end of the 20th Century to speculate on what life will be like at the end of the 21st Century, how close do you think he or she will be? I suspect the mark will again be missed by light years.

Just for fun, I ask my audiences, "How many of you think that 100 years from now the way people live will change, *but won't be all that much different from now?*" Usually about 30% of the hands go up. It's comforting to believe, "There's nothing new under the sun," because if the world doesn't change much, then there is little reason for a comfortable person to change much. It'll take 100 years to know if they are right, but their response reminds me of this quote from an intelligent individual jaded by change: "Everything that can be invented has already been invented." The person who uttered these immortal words? Charles H. Duell, Commissioner of the United States Office of Patents, in 1899. Apparently Mr. Duell was blind sided to the possibility of air travel, credit cards, and Post-it Notes. Despite the education and "street smarts" that helped earn his high position, Mr. Duell could not foretell the shifts in societal thinking that would be accelerated by Mahatma Gandhi, Walt Disney, Elvis, Bill Gates, and Mother Teresa — altering the way we express civil disobedience, relive our youth, enjoy music, compute information, and care for our brothers and sisters.

How much change will there be in your lifetime? I say, "LOTS!" Since the past is prelude to the future, take a look at what's new in recent years. This may give you a better feel for today's rhythm of change.

What's New Under the Sun?

If you were born before 1970, you were born before satellite TV, fax machines, digital beepers, cordless phones, space shuttles, disposable diapers, and earrings on businessmen.

You didn't have Nintendo, police radar, video rentals, microwave popcorn, VISA/MasterCard, nor cruise control. You came along before adult day care, caller ID, FedEx, CD's, ATM's, VCR's, MTV, and Chicken McNuggets.

Now, new in your life are palmtops, grocery scanners, computer viruses, Monday Night Football, sport utility vehicles, anti-lock brakes, air bags, and Wonder Bras.

For you, "gigabytes" and "modems" were outer space talk. Living together meant roommates. Smoking was cool, nobody fretted about cholesterol, and "mom, dad, I'm getting married!" implied to a member of the opposite sex.

Oh my, how the world has changed!

Are *you* ready for the changing world ahead? The writers of this book are successful consultants, speakers, trainers, and authors — plus we do a little philosophizing on the side. Cumulatively, having been inside thousands of organizations and having shared time with tens of thousands of people, we offer you some hard learned insight on success strategies for enhancing your health, wealth, and happiness. We believe where there's change, there's opportunity! Thanks for adding us to your personal support team.

DOUG SMART, CSP

Chapter 1

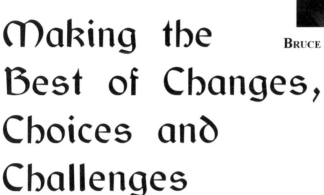

BRUCE WILKINSON, CSP

Making the Best of Changes, Choices and Challenges

We have all heard it before, "The one thing that is constant in life is change." I do not know when I first heard that statement or who first said it. I do, however, know that change is the one thing in life, like it or not, that will create opportunities and choices for the future. These "change opportunities" as I call them can take someone down several paths. That is why most changes in life are actually like a fork in the road. Some roads lead to opportunity, success, security, wealth and happiness, while others lead to danger, failure, financial ruin, loneliness and depression. The key is to know what road to take and the risk and reward that each road has along the way. Fortunately, many of the roads we travel have well-placed education and warning signs that can help us with our decisions. But as we all know, most accidents are caused by drivers who did not pay attention to the "warning signs" ahead. We also know that most bad drivers make poor choices and do not pay attention to the training and education that got them their license in the first place. It is my opinion that most of the training to handle change, or forks in road, comes from our parents and loved ones.

Making the Best of Change with What You Have Been Given

Okay, so we know that change is everywhere. But how can a business person or an entrepreneur use change to their advantage? The answer to this question is what separates the "best of the best" from the "rest of the rest."

Death brings unexpected change and choices.

I was only 16 when my father died of a heart attack in his sleep. Until then life was great! I came and went as I pleased; my mom cooked and washed, and I was living in what I now know is called a "bed and breakfast." Sort of like the one you are operating if you have teenagers — like my wife and I do. I even had long term goals; they were called weekends. You remember weekends. They are still in your calendar as an adult — but they are not as much fun. Of course that is our fault. But that is another story.

At first I felt sorry for myself. I was angry and felt it was unfair. How could my dad leave me as an only child with hardly any money to take care of my mother — who never found gainful employment? As I grew older and wiser, I discovered that my mom and dad had given me exactly what I needed to survive and thrive. My mom taught me manners, grace, humility, patience and to have a sense of humor. She also shared the importance of helping others, being well groomed, being polite, being a good listener, being creative and that enthusiasm is contagious.

My dad taught me perseverance, teamwork, how to overcome fear, anger, disappointment, staying focused and to be well grounded. He also shared with me the importance of having initiative, courage, a positive attitude, strong relationships and most importantly — it is all right to be a man and still be vulnerable.

Looking to the past to make the best of future change

No, my dad did not leave us a lot of money, and my mom was not able to make any more for us after he died. Yet I was able to survive and make the best of the first major change in my life because of the other riches my parents had given me. Here are some tips or road signs that will help anyone be prepared and make the best out of change.

- Realize that change will come and come often.
- Rely on the strengths that God, your parents, teachers, friends and mentors have given you to survive.
- Determine any weakness (such as decision making) you may have and seek help and education from

friends, family, colleagues, seminars or books to improve these areas as soon as possible.

- Create the mind set: with change comes an opportunity for success that may not have existed earlier. Some individuals actually utilize change to their advantage because it forces them to make a decision that for some reason they could not do on their own.

Making the Best of Choices and Challenges Due to Change

We know that changes will continue to be thrown at us and usually when we least expect it. So how do we know if we are handling change effectively? And how does someone know if they are making the best out of the changes in their personal and professional life? Easy, it is determined by the choices that we make based on the challenges due to change.

Where there's a choice and a challenge, there is an opportunity.

I was performing some training and consulting for one of my amusement park clients a few years back when 16-year-old Robert Williams showed up to apply for a job. He was one of hundreds of teenagers looking for work that summer (and most of them were only looking for work because their parents wanted them to). Robert was the oldest of four kids and his mom had recently passed away. The change in his life created the challenge of helping his dad take care of his younger brothers. Robert had come to his fork in the road where he had to make a decision. His choice was to stick with a part time job with a small construction company with little opportunity for advancement when he went back to school or to quit and gamble with an industry that he knew nothing about and had no experience in, although it had a reputation of providing some teenagers with a long-term career throughout high school and college. His mom instilled in him the need to provide an example for his younger brothers, and she wanted him to finish high school and attend college.

Where There's Initiative, There Are Possibilities (Or Success)

Robert decided to gamble, due partly because his highways had been marked with road signs of success by his parents long before he reached his first big fork in the road. Robert showed up in a three-piece suit and a briefcase. (That is right — a 16-year-old!) There he stood in the middle of summer in a hot suit among several hundred other teenagers wearing sandals, shorts, jeans, tee shirts, tennis shoes and halter tops. So, who do you think got interviewed first?

I asked if I could listen in on Robert's interview; after all, he was too good to be true. Mrs. Ryder of Human Resources said, "Good morning Mr. Williams." He said "Good morning Ma'am." You see, Robert told me later when you give someone respect they usually give it back. "What type of job are you applying for young man?" she asked. I have heard this question from Human Resource professionals in this industry many times, and I usually hear a selfish response about operating the best ride in the park. But not this time.

Robert said that "I would like to have whatever job that would make the guests happy so that they would come back again and spend more money." Wow! Robert had figured out why private sector employers were in business — to make money! When his interview was complete, I followed Robert out so that I could tap into his reasoning for what he did. I said, "Good morning Mr. Williams." He said, "Good morning sir." I explained to him why I was here and asked him what made him show up wearing a three-piece suit and a briefcase. He replied, "I knew that several hundred teenagers would not be wearing one." I asked him "what was in the briefcase" and he said, "I do not know — it is my dad's." I told him that we should open it. It contained some papers, his father's wallet, car keys, and beeper. I said "Robert, it's Saturday morning and you should go home quick before your dad wakes up." He replied, "Why?" I responded "So that you may live!"

Do you think that they hired Robert Williams? Do you think that they started him cooking hamburgers? Of course not. Not only did they hire Robert the next morning, but they trained him to assist in the screening process to enable the park to hire applicants that had been reading the same road signs that Robert had been seeing all of his life. Here are some of the road signs that Robert had read:

- Communication skills count.
- Perseverance pays.
- Enthusiasm sells.
- Listening skills show you care.
- Helping others is important.

- Having a positive attitude helps to sell yourself.
- Using humor shows confidence.
- Presentation skills make a difference.
- Have fun while you work.
- Humility is a virtue.
- Personal grooming and appearance are vital.
- Good manners are always appreciated and brings respect.
- Patience has its own reward.
- Teamwork is necessary for success.
- Risk taking is a means to getting ahead.
- Being creative puts you in demand.
- And above all — TAKE INITIATIVE.

As it turns out, Robert must have had the same parents (road crew), mentors, friends and loved ones some of us had.

So what happened to Robert over the next several years? The amusement park gave him a full time assistant's position in Human Resources when he graduated from high school, and they are paying for him to obtain his college degree at night. As you can see, Robert Williams definitely knew how to make the best out of changes, choices and challenges.

WHERE THERE'S CHOICE, THERE'S ALSO FAILURE

The Robert Williams success story is one that we all like to hear, and we hope that it happens to us. But sometimes we make choices that cause each of us to fail, and unfortunately, we must make the best out of these choices too.

It happened in my eleventh year as a speaking professional. I was presenting an opening keynote for an organization that had brought its managers to an off-site conference center. My client contact knew that I was half-Cajun and asked me to make sure that I included a lot of my humorous stories in my keynote. Something told me to think twice about this because this was a referral from another client and they had not really heard me present before. But I had done my homework, and they seemed to be a group that enjoyed humor. Unfortunately, I failed to communicate to the CEO personally that the humor would be coming from my Cajun heritage. It turned out to be a disaster.

Starting over with the fear of change.

About half way through my talk, the CEO stood up and demanded that I stop. He said that my type of humor was racist and that if I belittled my own heritage, then I would make fun of anyone's. My options, he said, were to finish my keynote without humor or to leave. I stood there motionless for over three minutes trying to decide what to do as the managers looked on with the CEO still standing. I thought about the risk that always existed by using Cajun humor in my keynotes but no one had ever complained before. After all, I thought everyone knew that Cajuns only make fun of other Cajuns. I thought about the mistake I had made in not telling the CEO even though my client in-house contact seemed okay with what I was going to do. I also thought about leaving, but that would go against all of the road signs that my parents had constructed for me. And finally, I thought about how I would cheat the audience of the worthwhile knowledge that I still had to deliver.

Deciding to change for the good of the moment.

After three minutes, (what seemed like an hour) I decided what to do. I stood up straight, cleared my throat and told the CEO that I would like to proceed. I also told him that I was not a racist and I apologized if I had offended anyone. I further explained about our fun loving Cajun culture and finished by saying that he could have handled it better by taking a break and pulling me to the side if he was uncomfortable. I knew at that point he could have kicked me out, but it would have to be his decision to make me leave and not mine. To my surprise, he sat down and did not say another word. I finished the program with very little humor but lots of enthusiasm!

At the conclusion of my program, the CEO would not shake my hand nor let me explain. My in-house client contact apologized to me and said that he still had some issues from the past that he was still dealing with. Boy, I could have used that information earlier. I also apologized to the other client who referred me since they too were represented in the audience. I later received several notes from managers who were in the audience who apologized for their CEO. As it turned out, I had to make a quick change for the good of the moment. It was full of choices and challenges, but with it came growth. My real decision was if I would leave all of my style of humor in for the same keynote that I was presenting the following week in a different city. I did a better job at my client homework, left most of the humor in and it was one of the best presentations of my career. It was also the presentation that I feared the most.

So in the end, I've picked up a few new road signs to add to my highway. They are "never assume," "integrity" and "recoverability." I know now that future roads will have multiple forks, roadblocks and crossroads and that each will bring choices and challenges. But I now also know that "where there is change, there is opportunity."

About Bruce S. Wilkinson, CSP

Bruce S. Wilkinson, CSP is a management consultant, motivational keynote speaker, workplace trainer and implementation specialist who reinforces personalized messages with both humor and enthusiasm. Bruce is a member of the Board of Directors of the National Speakers Association and is one of fewer than 350 people worldwide to earn the prestigious Certified Speaking Professional (CSP) designation.

As President of Workplace Consultants, Inc., he has developed and presented programs on effective leadership, communication, change, self-motivation, motivating employee behavior, humor at work, customer service, disciplining with dignity, substance abuse, safety and health, violence in the workplace and sexual harassment.

Contact Bruce Wilkinson, CSP:

Workplace Consultants, Inc.
1799 Stumpf Blvd., Bldg. 3, Suite 6B, Gretna, LA 70056
Phone: (504) 368-2994
Fax: (504) 368-0993
E-mail: SpeakPoint@aol.com

Chapter 2

Finding Firm Footing on *Shaky* Ground: Managing, Compensating, Attracting and Retaining Generation X Employees

BOB GOOGE

Have you noticed that there is something just a little different about your new young employees? Are your tried and true management techniques falling flat with this group? Welcome to the future!! No, your young workers are not from a different planet. They are the much talked about, written about, worried about, "Generation Xers." And in case you haven't noticed, they **are** changing the way America does business.

Who Are They?

Demographic information, which focuses on fertility traits, concludes that Xers are the folks born between 1963 - 1984. However, sociological information, which focuses on behaviors, concludes that the last baby boomer was born in 1960. For example: Sociologist's point out that a huge behavioral shift occurred in 1961 when, for the very first time, people took pills to keep from having babies.

Though the sociological and demographic information may be interesting, the real answer to the question "Who are they?" is that Xers are the employees who make you want to scream…

"Why don't they grow up and see the world the way I do?"

"Why do they always have to know why?"

"Can't they ever just do something because I told them to?"

Those cries of despair come out of the reality that Xers do not seem to be living by the same rules that pre-Xers live by. And the very first thing pre-Xers need to do to figure out who Xers are and where they are coming from is to shift some of our perceptions.

First and foremost — banish the phrase "Generation X" from your vocabulary forever. Exile it to the same place where you've stored the words "groovy" and "neat-o." The fastest way to antagonize an Xer is to call him or her an Xer.

The term we use at WOW! Performance Coaching is **Mold Breakers,** MB for short. MB's are breaking all the molds that used to work. Their entry into the workforce is causing decades of management, training, and compensation policies to be reevaluated or thrown out. For example:

Heather

Heather is your star computer systems wizard. She is 29 years old. Heather started working for you 18 months ago at $45,000 a year. You sleep well at night knowing that if the system crashes, Heather will go "above and beyond the call of duty" (or in this case $45,000 a year) to fix the meltdown. One day Heather walks into your office and quits. As you sit there stunned, Heather explains that she has decided to take a bicycle trip to the tip of South America. When she gets there she may stay for a few years as a computer consultant to the indigenous populations, or she might teach scuba — she hasn't decided yet.

Michael

Michael graduated with a 3.99 GPA in accounting, was president of his fraternity and every club on campus. Michael is the perfect college recruit. He is 23. You've been thinking that Michael might be due for a small promotion and raise in the next year or so, after he's done a bit more grunt work and paid a few more dues. But, exactly two years after you spent $10,000 recruiting him and $40,000 training him, Michael walks into your office and resigns. Why? He is tired of wearing suits and ties to work. So, he and two of his friends are starting an on-line computer-based accounting firm in the basement of their landlord's house. They already have five or six clients.

Laura

Let's not forget Laura, your personnel manager. Man is she good. She is rock solid, never misses a day of work. She is 32 years old, been with you for 4 ½ years. One day she walks into your office and quits. As you reach for the Maalox, Laura explains that she is going to work as a temp. She's tired of 50 - 60 hour weeks, and wants more control over her schedule. She thinks that a social life might be nice and, you know, maybe she might even want a family one day if work ever allowed her time to date.

All this happens in a 3-month period. You are losing your mind, some of your hair, or both. The exodus of talent is creating small explosions on your bottom line as your employee retention plummets. "What is wrong with these people?" you cry. "Haven't they ever heard of loyalty, responsibility? Don't they know that 60 hour work weeks are the norm in American business nowadays? Don't they know that (just like we did) they have to pay their dues, stick it out, (just like we did), before they make the big bucks, control their own time, or take a sabbatical?"

Oh, yes, they know all these things. The challenge for business is that MB's grew up in a different world than did Boomers. They survey the landscape from a very different vantage point that is alien to many of us.

The best way to see and understand the vast difference in world views is to hold those two worlds up side by side. Let's look at the cultural fault lines between Boomers and Mold Breakers. The social milieu of the 60s I have called the Revolution. This was the period of time when many Baby Boomers were coming into social awareness. The social milieu of the late 70s and 80s I call the Devolution. This is the time period when most Mold Breakers were waking up to the sights and sounds of cultural chaos.

Revolution
Boomers

1. Free Love
You may not have received any of this much talked about Free Love but even the idea of it had a powerful impact on the thoughts and attitudes of an entire generation.

2. Communal Action
The Revolution was time of civil rights and anti-war demonstrations. Prior to that, earlier generations rallied around wars and rumors of war to accomplish community projects. The idea of Community was a cultural value.

3. Sense of Improving Society and Social Optimism
The Revolution was full of people actually trying to live out the ideals of John F. Kennedy's Camelot, Lyndon B. Johnson's War on Poverty, and Martin Luther King's "I have a dream."

4. High Economic Expectations
During the Revolution there was actually a decrease in the gap between rich and poor. People thought that all Americans would share in any economic good fortune.

Devolution
Mold Breakers

1. AIDS
Love has never been free for Mold Breakers. It has always been a life threatening experience. In 1993 AIDS was the leading cause of death for Mold Breakers in 64 cities around the world.

2. Rabid Individualism
From a MB perspective it looks like any sense of community has been abandoned. Few seem to think that any one or any group can really change the system. Look around your neighborhood. Notice that people build back yard decks instead of front porches.

3. Sense of Dissolving Society and Social Pessimism — The
very first president that the oldest MB can remember is Nixon, who brought us the infamous Watergate scandal. This was followed by Carter's 21% inflation, 18% mortgage rates, and the Iran Hostage situation. The very first president who MBs could vote for was Reagan. Reagan rewarded all those 20-something votes with a 10 fold increase in the national debt, the benefits which went to boomers and those older. The tab is left to MB's.

4. Decreased Economic Expectations — This is the first
generation who will probably be financially worse off than their parents. Three-fourths of American college seniors say it will be harder for their generation to achieve the American dream than it was for the last generation.

Why? Inflation adjusted income for MBs has dropped 20% since 1979. Wages for new college graduates have decreased for 20 straight years when adjusted for inflation. And the average college graduate now has student loan payments that equal 24% of their take home pay.

The Revolution/Devolution model clearly shows why MBs and Boomers view the world differently. Now, why do you need to know all this? To manage MBs effectively you need to know the soil they grew up in. For example: Your world view may be that dues paying is part of corporate life. MBs view dues paying as a waste of time because they won't be around long enough to collect on the investment. Increasingly, those two world views are colliding.

Now, think about your MB workers who grew up in a Devolution environment. Note that this is not an environment of their choosing or making, but is simply the world they grew up in. What kind of work attitudes and behaviors would you expect from a generation who grew up in such a world? See if the following MB Profile seems on target.

Mold Breaker Profile

Mistrust of Institutions — All the institutions that MBs hear about that used to work, don't. **Government**, once a respected institution, is now demeaned and politically denounced as evil by the very people who make their living as politicians!

Schools produce graduates who can't read and can't get a living-wage job with their education. Schools have to beg from the community with bake sales, candy sales, shirt sales and numerous fund raisers. Even with all that, buildings are still falling apart, classes are overcrowded and teachers are stretched thin.

Businesses pay their CEO's multi-million dollar salaries, lay off thousands at a whack, cut the health care

benefits of workers to boost the bottom line and then
wonder why worker loyalty is lower than the Dead Sea.
There is more, but you get the idea!!

Fiercely Independent — in some sense MBs have always
needed to make it on their own. They are the latchkey kids
whose moms and dads practically invented the term "work-
a-holic." All this alone time creates an environment which
leads to poor communication skills and a real sense of
aloneness, making it difficult to connect with others. The
plus side of this is that MBs are very entrepreneurial. They
understand that job security with one company is dead —
85% of all new businesses in America are now started by
people under the age of 35.

Little respect for hierarchy — The hierarchy from their
perspective are the ones who engineered the mess they are
inheriting. They do, however, have an abundance of respect
for competency. A title means little to nothing, for an MB the
questions is "do you know your stuff?"

Very adaptable to change — Change is an MB's only
constant.

Incredibly Diverse — MBs are used to friends coming out
of the closet, becoming vegetarian, turning to Zen, piercing
their bodies, going new age. All this is simply regular life to
an MB.

Very Visual — Have you watched MTV? For thousands of
years humans have listened to music. Mold Breakers **watch**
their music.

So, how do you manage employees who think "Die
Yuppie Scum" sounds like a pretty good idea? You master
your **MB F.A.C.T.s**

F	**Fun**		**F**	**Flexibility**
A	**Acceptance**		**A**	**Ask Questions**
C	**Coaching**		**C**	**Communication**
T	**Training**		**T**	**Teamwork**

Fun — As children MB's experienced first hand the reality that 60 hour work weeks make mom and dad tired, grouchy and unavailable. For an MB a job is a means to end, not the end itself. They figure, "Hey, there is no reason why the place I spend up to 50% or more of my waking hours should not be fun." Study after study shows that as fun goes up so does creativity and retention.

Let me prime the pump a little bit on the whole *fun* issue — how about a David Letterman style Top 10 luncheon or staff meeting once a month? What about having a sound of the Day? The sound of the day is a noise chosen by a particular team member to signify a particular event. For example, a team member might bark when an order is ready to go out the door. The sound is for one day only. The next day a different team member gets to select the sound and what it signifies.

Why not establish a Joy Club? Joy Clubs are made up of team members who are responsible for making the workplace a fun enjoyable experience. They plan team socials, parties, make sure that people are recognized for accomplishments, birthdays, and are charged with making sure that joy is a daily part of work.

Fun at work is not illegal, immoral, or unproductive. MB's who are having fun at work are loathe to leave for another job.

Set your watch. For the next five minutes brainstorm ideas on how to make your company a more fun place to work. How could your job be more fun? How could you help your team have more fun. Don't put this off. Ready? Five minutes, go!

Now, take those ideas and pass them out at your next staff meeting. Sound silly? Good, you have the right idea.

Acceptance — The acceptance thing can be challenging, but — forget about the completely outmoded ideas of hair color, body piercing, dress codes. To MB's rules about personal style are an example of petty power games played by people who are more interested in hierarchy and conformity than competence. A willingness to live with some pink hair will gain you a lot of respect.

Coaching — The Hierarchy Model works like this — "This is what needs to be done, now do it." The Coach Model works a bit differently — "This is what needs to be done, now how can we get it done?" A key characteristic to remember is that MB's have a deep suspicion and low regard for hierarchy while they have a high regard for competency. If you are a good teaching manager, a good coaching manager, you will get their best work and you have a leg up on retention.

So, what does a good coach do?

A. A good coach gives specific instructions, sets specific performance standards, and is clear about each team member's responsibilities.

B. A good coach is firm when folks don't meet expectations or step out of line. MB's want feedback — even negative feedback. Remember that in many ways MB's are rookies. Prior to graduating from

college the only work experience they had was a
McJob. Don't jump to the conclusion that they are
trying to get your goat when they do something you
don't like. They simply may not know.

C. A good coach publicly praises his or her players for
a job well done.

D. A good coach manages to get the job done and still
have fun.

E. A good coach looks beyond the task at hand and
creates a vision.

Training — Training is your ace in the hole for retaining
MB's. More than any other employee group MB's tend to
make job decisions based on whether training is available.

MB's see themselves as self-employed even when they
are on your payroll. They know they have to build a career
based on skill, not a career based on a company. If you can
create an environment where MB's are continually adding
to their marketable skills, they will stick around to learn
more. When the learning is over, they are gone. So, keep
the training coming.

OK, so you're committed to continuous training. Now,
what does this training need to look like? Corporate training
used to be a "welcome to the family" sort of thing. However,
neither the nuclear family nor the corporate family still exists
as far as MB's are concerned. The family you're trying to
welcome them to is the same family that laid off their
parents. Instead of the family, welcome them to the *team*.
Focus your training on goals and results that show MB's how
they can and will contribute to the team.

When you start to design MB training, think multi-media
and experiential. Use computers, use animation, use role play

and all five senses like N.A.S.A. does in their astronaut training. Please keep in mind that MB's were raised on Atari, Nintendo and Gameboy.

MB training works best when it is "EnterTrainment;" when it is attention grabbing and entertaining.

Training and Development magazine conducted a Fax-Forum survey in May of 1995 asking MB's which training methods worked best for them. Not a single person said classroom training was the most effective. Not a single person said computer-based training was the most effective.

Ninety-two percent of the MB's who responded said experiential exercises are an effective means of training 20-somethings. Fifty-four percent of them said experiential exercises are the best training method followed immediately by games, facilitated discussions, and research.

In addition to asking them what style of training works best for them, MB's were also asked what kind of training they need. Here's what they said:

- **Basic-skills training**
- **Interpersonal-skills training**
- **Diversity training**
- **Quality or team training**
- **Computer skills training**

Especially when it comes to training, MB's have been accused of having short attention spans. Not true. What looks like a short attention span is really an ability to assimilate information quickly and from a variety of sources all at the same time. They process information by multi-tasking rather than linear association (**A** then **B** then **C**). To get a flavor for this watch some MTV commercials. There are usually four or five things going on at once. It may drive you crazy, but they are used to it and like it. If you train in the linear method MB's will be bored out of their minds, and yes their attention span will look very short.

Some final training words:

Focus — on end results, not welcome to family — but, "Here is what you need to know so you can contribute as part of the team."

Be Flexible — With smaller corporate work forces everyone is doing more. Give them options so they can fit training in with work, have some control over pace and place.

Emphasize Visuals — The media has trained us to expect a point to be made quickly and visually. Again go to MTV. MB's *watch* their music.

Continuous Training — For MB's this is seen as a must have for economic survival.

Flexibility — Companies have learned in the last decade or so that flexibility in marketing, and production is the new rule of survival yet little flexibility has trickled down into our work policies and procedures. Flexibility is a prime employment issue for MB's. Flexibility comes in many (flexible) styles:

Flexibility in time — Over and over again when I interview MB's I hear them say "We are not going to raise a nation of latchkey children. I want time off to volunteer, I can manage my own time." What would that look like in your organization?

Flexibility in compensation — Why assume that everyone wants to earn the same money for the same job? Maybe there is something else an employee wants more than money. Go ahead, be creative, think outside the box.

Here's an idea — What if your employee's jobs were centered around accomplishment instead of hours? Remember Laura, your ex-personnel manager? What if she had been given the option of working for accomplishment instead of hours? What if she got a 50-hour project done in 25 and you let her take the other 25 hours off! She might still be working for you.

What if after certain goals are met team members were rewarded with a 4-day week for a month. Multiple studies have shown that people who work a 4-day work week get as much work done as those who work five days a week.

Flexibility in dress — When I worked at Arthur Andersen & Company I had great flexibility in this area. I could wear a white shirt or blue shirt! Many of the stodgiest of companies now offer casual Fridays.

Flexibility means that you focus on results rather than time, appearance, and office presence.

Ask Questions — Get to know your MB's. Find out what they individually want to do. How do they want to do it? When do they expect to be able to do it? What kind of money do they want to earn? Is time off an issue with them? What do they do for fun?

The more questions you ask — the better. Here's an idea — use the *Book of Questions,* by Gregory Stock, Ph.D., at staff meetings once a week to give yourself an idea of who your folks are and what they think.

Communication — MB's are used to massive amounts of information delivered almost immediately. MB's expect over communication from a variety of sources using a variety of media — memos, bulletin boards (electronic and cork!), cartoons on doors, and e-mail.

Teamwork — MB's love teams if they are results focused. Remember that MB's see themselves as self-employed and want to build skills not kill time in unproductive team meetings. From an MB perspective teams need clear goals, deadlines, and responsibilities. Teams that exist only because teamwork is the in thing simply get in the way of an MB learning new skills or nurturing important relationships.

So how do you manage, compensate, attract, and retain MB's? You master your **F.A.C.T.s:**

1. *Fun, Acceptance, Coaching, Training*
2. **Flexibility, Ask Questions, Communications, Teamwork**

If you master your **F.A.C.T.s**, then one day you can expect one of your hotshot employees to walk into your office and tell you about the latest and greatest job offer she just had. Only instead of quitting she'll use it to tell you what a great company yours is to work for and why she's staying.

About Bob Googe

Bob Googe with WOW! Performance Coaching, Inc., brings a wide variety of skills and insights to MB Management. Bob was a CPA for Arthur Andersen & Co., Recruiting Coordinator for the Atlanta office of Andersen Consulting, consultant to Arthur Andersen & Co. on the creation and implementation of their North and South American "College Leadership Conferences," a co-creator of Service University, and a church youth worker. In addition to his WOW! Performance Coaching work Bob is also an ordained Presbyterian minister, and the Director of the Presbyterian Student Center at the University of Georgia in Athens, GA. Bob has written and presented extensively for both business and the church on the subject of Mold Breakers.

Contact Bob Googe:

WOW Performance Coaching, Inc.
10680 Loire Ave., San Diego, CA 92131
Toll Free: 1-888-WOW-YOU-2
E-mail: wowseminar@aol.com

Chapter 3

MIKE MONAHAN

Successful Change Leadership in Today's Workgroup Environment

Jack Welch, CEO of General Electric, once said, *"If the speed of change inside the organization is less than the speed of change outside the organization — the end is in sight."* In this book the various authors have made a compelling case for the need for positive change leaders. In looking at the greatest challenges associated with change, it is clear that helping groups through change is a special challenge. Let's review some facts about change:

All change produces feelings of uncertainty, ambivalence and anxiety in people. This is a universal feeling that has more to do with our humanness than our character or resilience. Psychologists tell us that any change is perceived as a threat to our well-being at a subconscious level. Even desirable change triggers this alarm response. This response may be very mild and remain generally unrecognized by the individual and unnoticed by others. This response may be an active, intense response resulting in tremendous feelings and observable behaviors.

People behave differently in response to change based on their readiness for the change and their ability to learn. In their work at the Center for Creative Leadership, Noer, Bunker and others have done extensive research into the change process and the effects of change on individuals and groups (Noer, 1996). Their findings indicate that an individual's *readiness for change* can be measured by looking at his stated opinions about change, his past history of adapting, the nature of the change (i.e., positive vs. negative), and the change-readiness of the organization. One can also measure an individual's *ability to learn.* Ability to learn is not an indication of intellectual capability as much as an indicator of the individual's adaptability, coping skills and previous experience.

- People whose ability to learn and readiness for change are higher tend to be early adapters or "Learners" as described by Noer. Learners are recognized by their willingness to feel challenged but be willing to try new ways. Learners produce results. Learners should be identified early and given "high impact" responsibilities in the change process.

- People with a high ability to learn but a low readiness for change are often active resisters in change movements and are described as "Entrenched." The entrenched have a strong need for encouragement and answers to the questions "Why?" and "What's in it for me?" Effective leadership tools for the entrenched include progressive work assignments with regular feedback, limits on resistance behaviors and modeling of success behaviors.

- People with a low readiness for change and a low ability to learn often have great difficulty in understanding the nature of the change and experience feelings associated with depression, such as a sense of dread, impending doom and wanting to flee. Noer describes them as "Overwhelmed." The overwhelmed are recognized by their withdrawn, disengaged demeanor. They often quit, request transfer or just show a lack of ability and interest. The overwhelmed need a supportive environment, reassurance and the opportunity to try new behaviors in small steps with close, personal supervision.

- An interesting category of people are those with a high readiness for change and a low ability to learn. They generally *appear* to be early adapters because of their positive outlook on change but, quite frankly, are hazardous to the success of change initiatives because of their inability to engage in appropriate adaptation behaviors. Additionally, these people may be a negative influence on others because of the dissonance between their stated readiness and their inability to perform. These people will be referred to as "Talkers." Talkers are hard to distinguish from learners in the early stages of the change process.

Generally, their performance does not equal their talk about their performance. Talkers need firm controls, specific performance requirements and controls on their ability to influence others. Talkers can make matters worse for the overwhelmed and entrenched. Learners can disengage from the change process when talkers are falsely recognized and rewarded.

Leaders can facilitate the adaptation to change through positive transition management. Rosbeth Moss Kanter has written that active opposition to change in the workplace is often the result of or worsened by the actions of leaders (Kanter, 1983). She states that recipients of change often resist for logical and predictable reasons. For example:

- Loss of Control — We do too much to people and too little with them.
- Too Much Uncertainty — We don't clearly light the way by revealing our plans and goals.
- Confusion — We create conditions under which people don't know what or how to do things right.
- Loss of Face — Just declaring the need for change makes people feel they look stupid for doing things the way they have in the past.
- Concerns About Competence — People have worries about their abilities to perform in the new environment,
- More Work — Change brings about the fear of too much work, requires more energy, time, meetings, etc.
- Ripple Effects — Change in one area affects and disrupts other plans and processes.

- Past Experiences — In the modern workworld, workers often have had multiple experiences with poor or failed change initiatives.
- Real Threats — Change can bring real pain and loss.

Even when we do everything right, there will be a certain amount of dysfunctional behavior that can derail the change process if not managed. For years, this author has struggled with the observation that even when everything "right" was done by change leaders, there was a strong likelihood that one would still have very difficult and surprising "people" issues to deal with, especially in groups. Dr. David Wadner, a clinical psychologist and renowned expert on group dynamics, describes a phenomenon in groups in transition called "Regressive Dependency" (Wadner, 1996). According to Dr. Wadner, a developmental task in any maturing adult is to be able to strike a balance between the need to be cared for by others — dependency — and the desire to disassociate oneself from others — isolation. The best psychological state for success in life and the workplace is to be <u>mutually interdependent</u>. People who have the ability to work well with others, yet still thrive in both "caring" and "cared for" relationships have the best set of skills for adapting to group needs, workplace demands and life. Dr. Wadner further states that when a workgroup is stressed, as in a high change environment, it is common for the members of the workgroup to regress to a greater state of dependency where the following conditions may result:

1. Instead of being satisfied with work, they act as if their work is to satisfy themselves.
2. Instead of thinking about their capabilities, they act incapable of thinking.
3. Instead of being responsible for their feelings, they feel they are entitled to act irresponsibly.
4. Instead of using emotions to guide rational thought, they let emotionality rule rationality.
5. Instead of tolerating diversity, they divert from tolerance.
6. Instead of setting boundaries on their impulsivity, they impulsively violate boundaries.

To produce a successful change initiative in the workplace today and to have an antidote to dysfunctional group behaviors such as regressive dependency, you must have change leaders. Leadership may be the *one key success factor* that will address the needs of the organization, the workgroups and the individuals in a changing work environment. Effective change leaders must be identified, nurtured and trained at all levels of the organization. Kanter describes a three-tiered approach to identifying change leaders (Kanter, 1983).

Top Level Executives and Managers — These titles carry the responsibility for being **change strategists**. Their job is to identify the need for change, instigate change and have a focus on the "Ends" of the change process.

Middle Managers and Supervisors — These titles carry the responsibility for being **change implementers**. They are responsible for being change project coordinators, overcoming resistance to change, translating strategy into action and have a focus on the "Means" of change.

Front-line Workers — These titles carry the responsibility for being **change recipients**. They are the users and adapters of new policies and processes. Their focus is on establishing congruence between personal needs and workplace requirements.

Successful Change Leadership

For any workgroup to master a significant transition, whether it's a clinical workgroup in healthcare, a manufacturing assembly line; professionals, clerical or retail workers, there are three imperatives for change success. These change imperatives are really under the control of those that are responsible for managing and leading these groups. The three imperatives are:

1. Alignment: Alignment means a consistent line of reasons for and acceptance of the purpose and vision of the organization (Gubman, 1998). Consistency between the ideas, goals and actions of the leaders of the organization, and the actual activities of the staff. The ability of the work processes and support systems to support those activities. Change can be a cause of misalignment in an organization or work group. Change can also be required to bring an organization into alignment.

2. Engagement: Engagement means we have to have our people involved in our business success processes and engaged in the process of the change

(Gubman, 1998). They have to not only be willing to rent their time and creative genius to us, but they also have to be willing to be engaged in the process of improvement, of telling us when we're doing things right and telling us when we're doing things wrong, and accepting and giving feedback. The "Great Paradox" of the group change process is just when we are most in need of the best effort and creative genius of our staff is just when our staff is inclined to withdraw or disengage from the process!

3. Measurements to Improve — There is an old maxim that states, "You can be winning but feel like you are losing if you don't keep score!" The reverse is also true. Change leaders must put measurement tools in place that carefully evaluate progress in both process and results. The most important factor is ensuring that measurements are geared towards the right variables and lead to improvements.

As a change leader seeking alignment, engagement and measurement, what steps should you take? How can you be successful? First, there are some questions to be answered:

1. What is to be changed?
2. Why is it to be changed?
3. What will be different after the change?
4. When and how fast should the change occur?
5. Will the change really work?
6. Who is for the change?
7. Who is against the change?

8. What kind of support will you get?

9. How will the change be announced?

10. Will everyone understand the change?

11. Is your timing for the change appropriate?

12. Will the change be perceived as beneficial?

13. How will you monitor the change?

14. Will the final outcome be worth the effort?

15. Is there another path that I should take?

Seeking Alignment

1. Number one in seeking alignment is: Have you clearly defined your **purpose**? This author attended a talk several years ago by the economist Arthur Laffer, who was Ronald Reagan's chief economist and was responsible for the "trickle down" economic theory that was described as the Laffer curve. The Laffer curve was the explanation for the anticipated but unrealized success of supply side economics. Arthur Laffer is a fascinating and engaging speaker. In this presentation, he advanced his theory that organizations that get in trouble, whether a big organization or a small department or workgroup, get in trouble because they act outside of their purpose. His examples demonstrated that organizations have a tendency to develop processes and support structures that do not contribute to the actual missions of the organizations. This, in turn, leads

to inefficiencies in operations, poor use of personnel and wasteful financial management. Laffer's main point was that organizations must be real clear about their purpose and that "purpose drift" may be an expected occurrence in any organization over time. When everybody knows what we're supposed to be doing, then it's much easier to determine whether or not we are doing it, to devote our resources to doing it, to support people who are doing it, and to make sure that it's getting done. As a change leader, you must make sure that those working for you are all in agreement about what your purpose is. Purpose creates an "intention to act," which is a very important predecessor to actually carrying out the action of your workgroup.

2. Second, you need to have **agreement** on how people will work together during and after the change process. You can't just assume that people come to work with good manners, an understanding of human behavior and ready to support each other. If these are things that you want, need, or expect to create the change you want in the work place, you have to have conversations about these expectations and get agreement. Getting agreement may be as simple as looking people in the eye and saying, "we've agreed that we're not going to talk behind each other's back. Terri, what do you think about that? Marcia, what do you think about that? Frank, what do you think about that?" The key is getting that level of agreement about very specific things related to how you work together.

3. Third, ask is there a **clear definition** of what is important? There are usually very specific reasons that

people don't perform up to the standards of the organization or their leaders. Workers will tell you one of the most common reasons for poor performance is that no one has ever made it clear what is <u>important to do in their job</u>. Those of us in the organizational development profession regularly come to workplaces and talk to front-line workers. A common theme is: "I'm real frustrated. I come to work, I work hard and do a good job, and then people tell me I should have been doing more of this or I should have been doing less of that. Why didn't they tell me that up front?" If we have general agreement in the workplace about what is important, and we, as managers, don't assume that our staffs know what is important, we would do much better in our quest for alignment.

4. Finally, have you defined the "rules of engagement" in the workplace? Defined rules of engagement means you must consider simple things like: how does your staff approach you as a manager? How do you as a manager approach your staff? Have you ever sat down with a staff member and said, "Here are signs of when I'm having a good day, and when I'm having a bad day. I prefer that you not talk to me about A, B, and C, on bad days but D is real important, so please come to me anyway?" Or, "Here are things that are really going to bring value to the workplace and are going to make me feel real good about the values you bring to the workplace." Or, "here are things that I expect to be challenged on." Consider your own workplace and generate examples of interactions related to rules of engagement. If those rules of engagement are defined and

spelled out, it makes it much easier for your staff to work together in a productive and cooperative way. Alignment will facilitate the change process.

Engaging your Staff

A staff that is involved in the processes and outputs of an organization will produce greater results. A staff that feels a personal commitment to producing results in keeping with the purpose of an organization is an engaged staff. Change leaders must take every opportunity to get their staff engaged in the change process to make the change successful.

1. Number one in engaging your staff is to <u>communicate</u> with your staff. Almost all managers express confidence in the way they communicate with their staff. They say, "Oh yes, I communicate with my staff. I have meetings with my supervisors and I pass all the information to them, and they pass it all on, and we publish a newsletter twice a month and it has all the information." "I'm real good about that; I have staff meetings once a week." Or, "I communicate all right. They know when I'm unhappy!" Amazingly, when you talk to front level staff, they almost always say their managers do not truly communicate with them. People want two-way communications. People want to be heard and understood. People want frequent and direct feedback on what they are doing well and how they can improve. Change leaders who explore the communication needs of their staff never find a person saying, "You know, you spend too much time telling me how well I'm doing," or, "You spend too much time telling me what's expected of me on the job," or, "You spend too much time

communicating what's going on here," — it doesn't happen. Focused, two-way communications will produce a staff more engaged in the change process and doesn't require a shift in organizational policy or money. Effective communications, especially in a time of change, can be critical to the success of the change implementation.

2. Second: Do you welcome suggestions, even if critical? A common occurrence is for workers to feel that they have little access to their leaders. Even access-friendly leaders are still perceived as arbitrary and sometimes vengeful decision-makers. Leadership decisions about promotions, work assignments and career futures have a dampening effect on open, upward communications. Staff are often reluctant to express anything related to something they want or something that might appear to be negative to their bosses. It's almost like having a bank account and making a withdrawal each time they talk to their manager. There is a pretty intense emotional feeling among people who have good ideas and <u>want</u> to be engaged in the process, but need to know if they have permission to express their ideas and concerns. Effective change leaders create an environment in which two-way communicating is a <u>performance expectation</u> and is practiced routinely.

3. Third: Do you find ways to enhance your staff? Do you give your staff training opportunities? Do you expect staff to learn new things? Do you engage in learning activities yourself? Do you share your knowledge and capabilities with people around you? These are important questions. You can actually increase the "ability to learn" quotient in your staff.

4. Fourth: Do you let everybody give his best? Edward Deming, the founder of the American quality movement, once said that "nobody comes to work with the intent of doing a bad job." Generally, the work environment, the quality of the leadership in the organization, and the work processes have the greatest impact on workplace quality and productivity. Getting your staff ready for and engaged in the change process requires an understanding of the forces of motivation. The number one motivator for people in the work force today is <u>feeling appreciated for the work they do</u>. How do you show appreciation? When do you show appreciation? Isn't the salary appreciation enough? Consider this, when you go to a restaurant and you get good service, even though you pay for the meal, you will usually say "thank you" to the wait person. If you see the cook on the way out, you say "thank you," because you appreciate what they have done for you, even though you've paid for the meal and service. If you show that same level of appreciation to those that work around you, for both their daily commitment and special achievements, you will increase their desire to produce positive results. The extra effort, stress and requirements of a changing environment make appreciation an even more critical engagement factor.

Measuring to Improve

As a change leader you must use tools to measure your results. Do not limit yourself to tools that measure work outputs only. Measure the change initiatives, acceptance of the change and determine how your staff is doing. Here is a very simple tool for getting a daily pulse on both work output and acceptance of the change. This tool can be used by change leaders and supervisors to monitor alignment and staff engagement. Ask your staff daily:

- ❑ "What worked well today?"
- ❑ "What made you feel good about working here today?"
- ❑ "What are you proud of today?"
- ❑ "Who deserves special recognition today?"
- ❑ "What didn't work today?"
- ❑ "What caused problems today?"
- ❑ "What made you angry today?"
- ❑ "What took too long or was too complicated?"
- ❑ "Are there any things that we did that took too many people or took too many actions?"
- ❑ "What did we have to do that didn't contribute to our purpose?"
- ❑ "What sorts of extraneous things did we attempt to do today?"

You will be surprised how often, at the end of the day, people feel pretty exhausted but aren't really sure what they've accomplished. Asking these questions indicates your desire to communicate and that you are interested in them. You create feedback opportunities for reassuring your staff and creating improvement expectations. Questions like: "What are you proud of today?" measures what we've done and sets the stage for people to take actions to be able to answer that question in the positive the next time you ask it. The question: "Who deserves special recognition for their accomplishments today?" helps us find those people who deserve special recognition. As a change leader, effective measurement of the change process requires an active search for results and opportunities for improvement.

Summary

In summary, the success of change initiatives with a group depends on many factors, but is most dependent on the leadership capabilities of those responsible for the change. Remember the following:

1. Change is inevitable and resistance is natural.
2. Maximized involvement means minimized resistance.
3. Don't create losers — or they'll get even.
4. Make certain the change supports your purpose.
5. Seek alignment, engagement and measure to improve.
6. Change strategists, change implementers and change recipients all have unique but equally important roles in change success.
7. Recognize and reward your "Learners." Support and encourage the "Entrenched." Develop and reassure the "Overwhelmed." Minimize the impact of the "Talkers."
8. Be prepared to use the antidote to "Regressive Dependency" — strong, positive leadership.
9. Separate from the past with a symbolic "ending" to the old way. Celebrate the new way.
10. Change requires *more* and *more intense* communication and follow-up than you might expect.

Bibliography:

Gubman, E. (1998). The Talent Solution: Aligning Strategy and People to Achieve Extraordinary Results. New York: McGraw Hill

Kanter, R.M. (1983). The Change Masters. New York: Simon and Schuster

Laffer, A. (1990). Speech to Meeting Professional International in San Diego, CA.

Lewin, K. (1951). Field Theory in Social Science. D. Cartwright (Ed). New York, Harper & Row

Noer, D. (1996). Breaking Free: A Prescription for Personal and Organization Change. San Francisco: Jossey-Bass

Wadner, D. (1996) Personal Conversations with Author

About Mike Monahan

Mike Monahan manages a consulting and training practice serving the learning and development needs of organizations in transition. Mike has worked as a clinician, manager and executive in several healthcare organizational settings. He has developed a particular interest in the needs of transforming organizations, focusing on helping teams and individuals improve performance and tend to the human side of change. Mike is a frequent speaker at national conferences and has consulting clients ranging from physician practices to Fortune 500 companies.

Mike's undergraduate degree is "With Honors" from the University of Colorado as is his graduate degree (Masters, Educational Administration and Supervision) from Roosevelt University in Chicago.

Contact Mike Monahan:

Performance Coach
1153 Bergen Parkway, Suite M-181, Evergreen, CO 80439
Voice and Fax: (303) 674-3186
Voicemail: 800-759-2881
E-mail: M2HRA@aol.com

Chapter 4

Five Steps for Making Life Changing Decisions

NICK NICHOLAS, CSP

There is nothing to be afraid of when it comes to change. You can control change when it comes. Before you say, *"What are you nuts?,"* let me tell you I am nothing of the sort. *There is nothing to be afraid of when it comes to change.* Somebody once said, "There are only two things you can be sure of in life: death and taxes." I think "change" should be added to that list. Change is constant. It happens every day. It is an ongoing part of our lives, like the weather. Yet I so often *react* to change with *fear.* In this chapter, I will show you how to confront that fear. I will show that *there is nothing to be afraid of when it comes to change,* because while we *can't* control when change comes, we *can* control our response to it.

From the moment we are born, change is an ongoing part of our lives. When we're infants, we are the objects of our mother's undivided attention until little brother or sister comes along. As toddlers, we think we have it made until we board our first school bus to kindergarten. As teenagers, we fall in love for the first time, and then, when we least expect it, change happens. Our partner — the one who promised he or she would love us forever — says "Hey, it's been nice," and moves on to someone else.

We move from one grade to the next until we're out of high school. At graduation we cry and yell, and for most of us, we move onto college. Some of our friends move with us, others don't. We change jobs voluntarily and involuntarily. We do the same with plans, goals and schedules. We have children, and they grow up, one year at a time, changing constantly.

When audiences hear this, they say, "Well, most of those are expected and controllable changes. We have opportunities to figure out what to do, and we can then make decisions based on those opportunities. We are more in *control* of what happens. But when we have unexpected changes...."

When it comes to change, control is everything. The more we control, the less we fear. And we can control more of what we think we can't control by *responding* to change rather than *reacting* to change. The difference between *responding* and *reacting* is in how we arrive at the decision on what action to take. *Reacting* is an involuntary decision based on emotion, usually fear. *Responding* is a voluntary decision based on knowledge, thought, research and debate. Our control over change, and the fear of the unknown that it generates, lies in understanding how to make logical *responsive* decisions rather than involuntary *reactive* decisions.

In a recent book I coauthored with Steve Cohn, *Finding the Magnetic Leader Within — Moving From Personal Chaos to Personal Peace*, I layed out a five-step process, R.E.A.L.M., for handling the emotions generated by change, especially fear, so we can focus our energies on the opportunity offered by change. The following story about my Vietnam experience illustrates how responding to change can overcome fear and give you control over the changes you encounter:

In the late 1960s I found myself, like many others, in the Army and going through training to prepare me for a tour of duty in Vietnam. That special training would provide me with a "life lesson" that would serve me well in the years ahead.

We were working as three-man reconnaissance teams. We carried the least amount of equipment and rations possible and were taught to live off of the land and avoid being captured by the enemy. However, we were also taught the skills to handle being captured and to endure the rigors of interrogation and torture.

I remember one of the instructors saying, "In combat, everything is changing every second, and you had better learn to deal with tough changes. But you better believe that no change you will ever face can equal the change you'll experience when you suddenly find yourself in the hands of an enemy — an enemy who controls everything that happens and who could care less if you live or die… as long as they get what they want from you."

After several days of intense training we were given the opportunity to put into practice the skills they had given us through a three-day escape-and-evasion course. We were given our allotment of equipment and rations and a hand-drawn map of the course. The objective was to move from the starting point to the finish line, gathering and reporting information back to our base unit. The catch was we had to accomplish the mission while facing an aggressor force comprised of former North Vietnamese soldiers who had changed sides after being captured.

The North Vietnamese soldiers' role was to make our job as hard as possible and to capture us, if possible. If they captured us, we would be taken to a prison camp run by the Vietnamese aggressors. There were no Americans in the aggressor force or in the prison camp.

In the first two days, our team was moving through the course very well. We had collected a lot of information, and even though we had seen the enemy, we hadn't been seen. By late afternoon of the third day, we were less than two miles from the finish line and, knowing we had until midnight to finish, we decided to move to the edge of a heavily wooded area about 200 yards from the finish. We would then wait for the cover of darkness to advance across the grassy open area between the woods and the road which was the finish line.

When darkness came we realized there was a flaw in our plan. For the first time since we started out, there was no cloud cover. There was a full moon flooding the whole area in a bright light. We could see and hear soldiers of the aggressor force on the road standing around their trucks laughing and talking. We decided they were sufficiently distracted for us to quietly crawl through the high grass and to the road without being seen. We had gotten about half the way across the clearing when one of our guys let out a loud sneeze. We froze.

Within seconds they were on us. I felt a boot come crashing down on my neck as I lay there, trying to be invisible.

Then I was being yanked to my feet. My hands were tied behind me, and a blindfold was put over my eyes. The two soldiers were yelling at me in Vietnamese, and I didn't understand a word. They dragged me to one of the trucks, turned me face down and threw me into the back of the truck like a sack of potatoes.

The instructor's words about being captured came back to me. But so did his message about what to do if it happened. "Remember," he had said, "that even though you may feel out of control, there are two things you cannot lose sight of. The first is that any change — even something this harsh — offers both opportunity and consequence; do not let the shock of being captured force you to focus on the negative consequence, but focus on looking for opportunities to escape. The second is that you may not control what is going on around you, but you *do* control the decisions you make regarding how to handle it. You only lose that power when you give up hope. The bottom line is *never give up hope* and *always focus on the opportunity* of escape."

They put us in individual cages far enough away from each other that we could not communicate with each other. After about four hours of sitting in my cramped cage, they took me out into an open area inside the compound. The interrogator got right up in my face as I was being held by two soldiers and, in broken English, began yelling questions at me.

I kept replying with name, rank and service number. He grew angrier and angrier. Finally he looked me right in the eye and said he knew a way to make me talk. By now it was well after midnight, and I was so tired and scared that frankly I wondered if he might be right.

The two soldiers dragged me across the compound to a freshly dug hole in the ground. It was about six feet long, two feet wide and two and a half feet deep. The interrogator asked if I was afraid of snakes and rats. I was terrified of snakes. If I spoke he would hear it in my voice, so I remained silent.

He pushed my head over so I could look into the hole. As I stood there, my heart stopped and my legs turned to rubber. There was a wooden box constructed to fit the hole snugly with its top about four inches below ground level. In the box were several snakes and what looked like three medium-sized rats.

My intellect was trying to tell me that this was *a training exercise* and that these people were not going to seriously hurt or kill me. But my belief system was incapable of accepting that as fact.

Suddenly, the two soldiers were tying my feet together. They forced me into the box, then they placed a lid on the top. It had a small square opening covered with screen wire. I heard dirt being thrown on the box and felt the snakes crawling over my neck and arms. The interrogator looked through the opening and fired a few questions at me. I was so scared that I was just about to tell him anything he wanted to hear. But I remembered the instructor's message about opportunity and consequence and focus.

He said that the best way to keep focus on the opportunity is to keep a positive attitude. That, he said, was best accomplished by thinking about people, places and events that we enjoy. He told us that when we are out of control, we need to remove ourselves from the situation, and think of something exciting and pleasant. It will keep your attitude positive so you can focus on the opportunity to escape. So I decided to remain silent.

I began to think about the last weekend I had spent in Seattle, the fun I'd had and the girl I'd met that weekend. Then I started singing the "Star Spangled Banner" from front to back and then tried to recite it back to front. After that I said the "Lord's Prayer" forward and backward.

Meanwhile, the interrogator was yelling questions and threats at me. I was completely unaware of his presence, which made him madder and madder. Finally they took me out of the box. Later I discovered that I had been in there for 45 minutes.

The interrogator then put me in a small tent, where I suppose I should have slept. By now it was very early in the morning, and a heavy overcast had rolled in, obscuring the moon and making it extremely dark. I felt a great sense of pride in my accomplishment and a sense of relief for having my feet untied. I heard the guard begin to snore. This was my chance!

Quietly, I began to slide under the back edge of the tent and down the incline behind it. When I was about 20 yards down the hill, I jumped to my feet and ran. As I did, I kept hitting trip wires that set off flares. The sky began to light up with the flares, but I kept going. Finally I was far enough away that I felt I could stop and take a breather.

I listened closely. Hearing nothing, I decided that they must have given up the chase. About midday I was picked up by a team of exercise referees. I felt fantastic and proud. I had been captured, kept my head, used my training and survived to escape and fight again another day. All of this was the result of my decisions to *respond* rather than *react* to the situations I faced.

My experience teaches us a lot about change and the opportunities it offers if we make logical responsive decisions rather than involuntary reactionary decisions. Especially when we face enormous fear. There were several decision points in the story but the one that generated the most fear for me was being in the box with the snakes and deciding whether or not to give the enemy any information. I was faced with reacting to the fear I felt, thus giving control to my captors, or collecting my thoughts, applying my knowledge thus allowing me to control my response to the situation and ultimately escape.

Let's look at the decision making chain. When faced with a situation two things happen immediately. First we experience an emotion and second we are presented with several courses of action to chose from. We then select a course of action and take action.

Whether the decision is responsive or reactive, the decision is determined by how we handle the emotion generated by the situation. If we recognize and process the emotion, the decision will be *responsive* based on thought, knowledge and logic. If we fail to recognize and process the emotion, the decision will be *reactive* based on the emotional feeling of the moment. In reactive decisions our knowledge and logic are used after-the-fact as a means of rationalizing our action.

The R.E.A.L.M. process, when used as part of the decision making chain, provides a way to handle the emotion generated by the situation.

So with that in mind, let's take this part of my experience through the decision making chain and the five step R.E.A.L.M. process.

The moment those guards placed me in that box with those snakes, my fear level soared to near panic. Immediately, I was presented with several courses of action. I could give up and tell them what they wanted to know, or I could give into the panic and start screaming and yelling hysterically. Either of these courses of action would have given them more control over me and placed me in even greater pearl. My third option was to apply what I had learned, take control of my situation and hold out until I could find a way to escape. Unfortunately, the third option wasn't an option unless I could get past the enormous urge to give in to my fear, tell them what they wanted to know and get out of that awful place. This is where the R.E.A.L.M. process comes into play and here is how it works.

R = Recognize/Refocus: *The step gives us insight.*
Our insight comes when we recognize:
- How we feel about what is happening.
- That we are focused on the negative emotion of the situation.
- What opportunity the situation offers.

This step is critical because "energy follows focus." If our focus remains on the negative emotion, we continue pumping energy into that emotion until we are driven to select a course of action that relieves our emotional discomfort. If we refocus on the positive emotion generated by the opportunity, we pump energy into that emotion until we feel much better about ourselves and the situation. This allows us to stop — collect our thoughts — review our knowledge of the situation — apply logic and select a course of action that addresses the situation appropriately. When we have recognized the need to change our focus from the negative to the positive, we can then use the next four steps of the R.E.A.L.M. process to accomplish the refocusing of our energy.

Applying the Recognize Step

Immediately, I became aware of just how scared I was and I realized that all I was thinking about was being bitten by the snakes or suffocating in the tight confines of the box. Then I remembered what our instructor had told us, "Do not allow yourself to focus on the negative consequences of the situation, you must focus on the opportunity to escape." What was the opportunity to escape? Then it hit me, if I could hold out and not give them information they would have to find another way to force me to talk. That meant taking me out of the box and moving me somewhere else, and that process just might give me the opportunity to escape.

What is your box? What animals or ghosts bring out the fears that influence your decisions? Whether it's a job you're not happy with, a relationship that isn't working or a feeling that life is overwhelming you — stop. Recognize how you feel about the situation. Check to see if you are focused on the negative emotion and then identify what opportunity this situation offers. Remember that you are not a victim of the winds of change — you have choices. Do not fear tomorrow because tomorrow is the result of the decisions you make today — and you control those decisions. Be responsive not reactive in your decision making and you can escape the situations that are holding you back. Then your life can be what you want it to be!

E= Eliminate Blame: *This step gives us control.*
This step is very important because we cannot refocus from the negative to the positive unless we have control over the emotions we are feeling. We gain this control by taking responsibility for how we feel. The act of blaming transfers that responsibility to someone or something else. And when responsibility is transferred, so is control. In essence, when we blame other people or things we give them control over how we feel and our focus remains on the negative aspects of the situation.

Applying the Eliminate Blame Step
As I laid there in that box, there were many people and many things I could blame for what I was feeling. If the stupid moon had not been shining I wouldn't have been captured. If the guy who sneezed had of just kept quiet we would have made it to the finish line. If my captors weren't such cruel and insensitive people I wouldn't be in this box. This list could go on and on, but the reality was that every time I blamed someone or something else I was giving away my control. One of the things that all of my Army training had continually drilled into me was that I had to be responsible and accountable because failing to do so could cost a life, maybe mine. Right then I realized that I was responsible; not the moon or the other guy. Granted there were other factors that played into my capture, but they were events of circumstance that I didn't control. And these events did not relieve me of my responsibility.

Who or what are you blaming for how you feel? Are you holding your boss responsible for how you feel about your job? Do you see the other person in your relationship as the one who makes you feel the way you do about the relationship? If the answer is yes, then you are giving them control over how you feel and of your decisions. Take responsibility — stop blaming — be in control.

A = Accept: *This step gives us permission to stop blaming.*

This step is critical because without it we will not be able to stop blaming. To stop blaming we must accept that how we feel is okay and where we are at this moment is where we are supposed to be. This is accomplished by accepting that everyone involved, you included, made the best decision possible based on the information available at the time. And that the events that took place happened for a purpose.

Applying the Accept Step

I had become unaware of the interrogator yelling questions at me and cursing me for answering with name, rank and service number. I had accepted that blaming someone or something for what I was experiencing was a dead-end road leading to disaster. I had accepted responsibility for what I was experiencing and that gave me strong sense of control.

Have you given control of your life to someone or something else? Do you want it back? It's yours for the taking if you will stop blaming and accept that the person you are holding responsible made the best decision they could based on the information available at the time. Also, accept that at this moment you are exactly where you are suppose to be, because the situation is affording you the opportunity to learn something you need to know. Accept responsibility and take control.

L = Learn: *This step gives us knowledge and wisdom.*

The sense of control gained by accepting responsibility calms the emotion allowing us to logically review the knowledge we currently have about the situation and to determine what additional information is needed before we make our final decision. This step also gives us a second learning opportunity. That second learning is wisdom. Wisdom is what we learn from having experienced the event. It is what we can apply to other situations as we go through life.

Applying the Learn Step

Now that I was feeling a strong sense of control, I was able to logically review the knowledge I had and what I needed to learn to make a sound decision about my situation. I remembered the instructor saying to us, "As a prisoner, you may find yourself experiencing both physical and emotional pain, brought on by some form of torture. It will be easier for you to endure the pain if you can mentally remove yourself from the situation." I immediately applied this knowledge by mentally going back to that great weekend in town. By doing this, I learned that the longer I ignored the interrogator the more distraught he became. He was obviously frustrated that his attempts to intimidate me into talking weren't going to work. Armed with this additional knowledge, my resolve to keep it up deepened. I became confident that he would give up soon, remove me from the box and find some other way to extract the information.

I didn't know it then, but looking back I realize that from living through that experience I learned many things. I learned that no matter how dark the situation may seem, there is always an opportunity. I also learned that if you identify what you want, focus on it and refuse to give up hope, it will be yours. That's wisdom.

What knowledge do you have about your situation? What additional information do you need to make a sound and logical decision? Accept responsibility for what you are experiencing, learn as much as you can about the situation and apply that knowledge to logically select a course of action. Remember, tomorrow is the result of today's decisions. In other words — you do control tomorrow.

M = Move-On: *This step gives us confidence, peace and calm.*

Even after a situation is resolved, the emotion often lives on impacting our decisions. For that reason, this step is very important. Though we will never completely erase the event from our memories, we can neutralize the emotion with which it is associated. This frees us from the past and allows us to move forward with confidence, peace and calm. There are many ways of neutralizing emotion. One that I have found to be very effective and nonviolent is to write it down, talk it out and let it go method. Here's how it works.

Sit down and write a letter to the person or thing that has generated the emotion you are feeling (this letter is not to be delivered.) Express how you feel using words that are very descriptive and specific. When the letter is finished, either read it aloud to yourself or read it to someone close to you that can keep a confidence. Once the letter has been read aloud, you have subconsciously given yourself permission to let it go. Sometimes it takes more than one letter to let go of the emotion.

Applying the Move-On Step

I carried the emotional scars of this event for several years after it happened. Ultimately, through a concerted effort and several very descriptive letters, I was able to let go of the emotion. Today, as I write about it, I relive it in my mind, but there is no emotional reaction. It can no longer negatively impact the decisions I make.

Remember, the past is past. Holding onto emotions from the past affects the decisions you make today. When this happens, you remain in your box.

Change is not optional in today's world. What is optional is how we decide to approach it. We can make involuntary reactive decisions that give control of our lives to others, or we can approach it with courage and confidence, taking control by making responsive decisions based on knowledge and logic. Control our lives, or give control to others. The decision is ours.

About Nick Nicholas, CSP

Nick Nicholas is an internationally recognized speaker, trainer and consultant. His enthusiasm, content, and humor have excited audiences from Boston to Bangkok and Seattle to San Juan.

During his 35 years experience in sales, leadership, and change management, he has developed a unique understanding of how people deal with change, both personally and professionally.

He now travels the globe sharing these insights. He is dedicated to helping organizations turn rapid change into rapid growth by harnessing the power of change and creating a powerful focus which will propel them into the 21st century winners circle.

Nick is also the author of an influential book on personal change entitled, Finding the Magnetic Leader Within — Moving from Personal Chaos to Personal Peace. His client list includes Hewlett Packard, Owens Corning, Oldsmobile, Turner Broadcasting, the IRS, Amoco Oil, Saturn, The American Legion, and bank associations in over 30 states.

He is a member of the National Speakers Association and has earned the coveted Certified Speaking Professional (CSP) designation.

Contact Nick Nicholas, CSP:

ProMax and Associates, Inc.
3999 Austell Road, Suite 303-362, Austell, GA 30106
Phone: (770) 439-8900
Toll Free: (800) 925-5788
Fax: (770) 439-8909
E-mail: nicknicholas@writeme.com

Chapter 5

It's Your Turn to Bat!

DEBRA WASHINGTON GOULD, MS

Yes, we are talking about *Change Management*. Change is good. This kind of change management relates to your human spirit and stepping out on faith. The decision to change from within starts with your belief in you. Instead of talking about the organizational *change* with a corporation, we will focus on the human belief system. You can arrive at this station in life only after you have been pushed to the limits. We know that change management deals with time and how it will impact our future. But what about your future endeavors? Have you put them on hold to satisfy other people's goals? I was that kind of person who lost sight of her own ambitions and desire to become an entrepreneur. It was mostly as a result of my own fears to take a risk in myself. On this particular day, I sat at a baseball game, watching my son's team playing with excitement and fun. I sat there not having much fun even on my own time. I said then something has to change, and it *must* start with me. How and where do I regain the momentum and focus to get on course?

Do you ever feel like you keep hitting foul balls when you are up to bat, on the job, at home, in your relationship or extended family and friends? My chance at bat related to being at work. I knew that I was the only person holding me back. It was up to me to pick up the bat. The opponent talents on the other team were not much better than my own skills. It was me blocking my own blessings — and my lack of confidence to do something about it. So, let me explain my situation, and maybe this experience can help you go through your own change-management processes.

Whether you are working for a major Fortune 500 company or a small company, there is change around us every day. The key is preparedness — having your own dream worth waking up to everything. How do you fit in the plan impacting your future? Are you willing to change or rather to remain status quo and not rock the boat? Does your company management ever ask your opinion about what you think? How do the computer technology and the work flow affect your performance? What are the changes occurring in your organization which impact the demands at your desk or work station? I discovered for myself that no one really cared about what I or my peers thought. We were the grunt workers and it didn't matter. The harder I worked to make a difference, the less it mattered. For most women in the project management professional and technical field, we kept hitting the brick wall; the glass ceiling didn't even exist.

There were several aspects of change management from a human interest point of view. After watching my son's baseball game one night, I related several things in my organization that I associated with baseball. Just think of yourself hitting the ball and getting to first base. The next hitter has to get you to the second or third base. Earlier, I said change is good; however, it is not easy because of the culture and mind set of the company. Let me explain some of the hurdles and unexpected surprises that occur in the midst of change. I am choosing a human-interest viewpoint because *change* comes from within you. To see positive *change* you must go through the pain of *change* to see growth. When we think of change management for your success, happiness and achievement, you get there through determination, persistence and overcoming obstacles. Somewhere in life you experience pain. Let's think in terms of playing baseball.

You are a corporate employee and ready to position yourself to bat. You are up first to bat. You're up first because your company management constantly reminds you that you are a team player and outstanding achiever with strong work ethics — a confident, and conscious-minded employee. With all of this going for you, you think only about winning all the time and maintaining a positive attitude. There is no one on base. The company is experiencing a reengineering. You have initiated an interest to participate on the reengineering team. You're thinking, *I want to be actively involved with the processes of finance, management information system, engineering, operations, training, property, procurement, and legal* to keep abreast of the new wave of information flow impacting your company. You're thinking, *why not me?*

The first base is the work environment. You have been chosen to serve on the reengineering team. The CEO assembles the focus groups and explains the critical impact of your important role and changes affecting the company. The vision, mission statement, goals and objectives set for every department are very crucial to the long-term growth of the company in order to survive these changing times. Well, you're thinking, *I want and will make a difference.* This focus group may be worthwhile, after all. The CEO conversation shifts a little from the impression of team. The surface conversation sounds non-committed by senior management. As usual, you know that it will be the worker bees pushing the *change* down to the workers. You hear a smooth pep talk on how the economy dictates the United States take on leadership to hold onto their Big Brother image to foreign countries, that major corporations have to do their part in bringing businesses back to the United States. We cannot get there without the loyalty and teamwork of this company's employees. Those who understand what is ahead will definitely survive the *change* in times. It all sounds great, but management expects a commitment from its employees. The conversation keeps drifting away from what's in it for the employees. Are there any lump-sum bonuses, salary compensations, or means of incentive awarded to those hanging on?

I had personally come to a decision that it would be worthwhile for me to participate in a focus group. Overall, the company's health plan and retirement benefits were compatible with leading industry's types. My husband and son depended on my portion of our financial security. I sat there, trying to convince myself that this reengineering change was for the betterment of everybody. In my final assessment of this meeting, did I or anyone else matter at all? So what if I accepted the change or not?

Something was wrong with this picture. The pep rally continued; computer technology would replace those workers who were not working to their potential. The board of directors recommended a larger share of the return on investment from their corporation. The *change* in times had caused management to consider early retirement, like in so many other companies. It would be inevitable, but there were some who would experience reduction in workforce. Just listening to all of this drama makes me wonder why I decided to serve on the reengineering team. Is it because I wanted to hear firsthand this horrible and terrible news? I see that my work is cut out for me.

Remember, I am up to bat. I hit the ball right past the short stop and managed to get on first base. Remember, the consultant firm was under a reorganization. The CEO announced that there must be higher productivity with fewer employees. Every senior and middle management employee was given the charge to determine who are the quality and productive employees to survive this reengineering. Those of you serving on focus groups have been privileged to receive company-sensitive information. Now the middle managers are tasked with stepping up to the batter's box. Does he decide to do the right thing to choose quality employees whose strong work ethics will make a difference? Or does he operate from the "good ol' boy" culture and take care of his buddies?

I am on first base watching this person squirm with fear. The first two swings are foul balls. He is feeling the pressures of *change* in doing the right thing and to select qualified staff in his functional area. He finally hits the ball, and I run to second base. I made it to the second base. The middle manager is looking weary and vulnerable. What does this mean for his future or my future, i.e., to have chosen a qualified and strong African American woman over his buddies? The middle managers have all done their homework to select key players for the transition. They now have to report their results to senior management. There is a company wide meeting by senior management to offer the voluntary separation package across the entire company. There were some employees encouraged to sign up. Anyone refusing will take the risk of reduction-in-force (RIF). What time of day is it? Who's on the base? Survival of corporations' *changes* to reduce headcount through RIF or early retirement brings on tension and enormous anxiety.

This was a devastating *change* that broke down the culture of the good ol' boy syndrome. *Change* in the economy demanded superior performances. The competitive market even penetrated the choices of management to do the right thing. They were forced to deal with reality — the *change* that a new and diverse work force necessitated quality work, business ethics, strong work ethics and team players. No more protecting the troublemakers who refused to work in a cooperative spirit. No more waste, fraud and abuse of company resources to take care of just a few.

Progressive *change* in the reengineering process meant all learners had an equal opportunity to be trained and quickly utilize this application knowledge immediately in their work areas. If you were provided the training, it was your responsibility to share information and start training your peers as well. The *change* was different in the work force because some people can learn and perform a task but not everyone is a trainer. For the first time in many years we had a functional work environment and professional types who were willing to work together and share information. The atmosphere was now conducive to work in harmony in a cooperative spirit with a renewed team approach.

The new regimen phased out after several months. We didn't return to the old ways, but the stress and intensity increased. This new work flow created longer work hours. A regular eight-hour workday, or 40-hour workweek became a thing of the past. The workdays were longer now, a typical day at work on an average day was 12 hours, without overtime pay; sometimes it was 12 to 14 hours a day, with 30 minutes for a lunch break. There were no discussions by management to decrease the workload nor salary incentives. Those who survived the RIF or early retirement packages were now unhappy campers and suffered from exhaustion. What did this type of *change* translate for our future? The tension was building, and the office politics plagued the work environment, with the typical rumor mills, complaining and blaming; performance levels of outstanding employees were being questioned. Fingers pointed, and no one wanted to accept accountability or the responsibility to lead anymore. The work environment was getting hostile.

Here I was stuck on second base — doing all the right things to support senior and middle management — and there were no *change*s in job advancement or more money. I was ready to change again. I wanted off of second base. I decided to look over my employment options. I was feeling stifled and stagnated on the reengineering team. The focus groups were meeting often. The heavy workload at my work station didn't go away while I was serving on a focus group. We were losing interest and focus about the company and its new *changes.*

I started thinking a lot about my own business startup. After much deliberation and talking to my spouse, network friends and peers, I decided to take the plunge. I set out a course of action to leave. It was two years later before I finally reached this decision to leave. I kept reviewing my goals, writing down my vision of what the future should look like for Debra Gould & Associates, LLC. I continued to review my options by committing to paper the advantages and disadvantages of my business startup. The more I went to work, the more I hated my job. The day I finally realized it was time to go, I said**, "Your Turn At Bat,"** and I never looked back again. Everything about this *change-management process* involved my human spirit, forcing me to be vulnerable and scared most of the time. But one day I just said, *to myself, feel the fear and do it anyway.*

The next hit ball went to the right fielder, and I ran to third. Now the bases were loaded. I was looking at my senior manager, who was the only person that decided whether I would receive a hefty increase for working long hours and extremely hard over the years. Would he even consider allowing me the proper training to proficiently manage my priorities? He was delaying decisions to hit the ball. He struck out. He made the decision easy for me: I decided to leave. I decided on February 12th, Lincoln's Birthday. This anniversary date would be a permanent reminder of Emancipation Day — a day of *freedom.*

Believe it or not, the day I decided to leave was a rejoicing day. There was a unique transformation happening. I discovered there were a lot of things people believe in doing, whether it is a minor or major thing happening in their life. We talk and talk about it to everyone who is willing to listen. We manage to convince ourselves that the perfect time will come to make a *change*. There is no perfect time for *change*. I got to weigh all of my options. I tried to talk myself out of starting this business venture. I had others to consider before I choose to impact the family's financial security. The day I removed all of the drama about why I couldn't take this risk, I found out that once I moved myself out of the way, the floodgates started pouring in blessings, ideas, sponsorship, opportunities; my advocates and supporters began to accelerate their efforts to reach out and help me.

I discovered that people believe in a lot of things, but until you step out on faith there is no *real* change management. All *change* is within you. Even with this armed faith and knowledge, I still have had my share of obstacles and roadblocks. It's too late to worry now. So, I look ahead with courage, determination and persistence, and I do what I fear most. I tell myself that I never see failure as failure but as an opportunity to learn and grow. Am I afraid to take risks? Yes, but I feel the fear and do it anyway. So "It's your turn to bat!" Go for it!

About Debra Washington Gould, M.S.

Debra Washington Gould is an inspirational speaker, management consultant, and trainer based in New Orleans, LA. She is the president of Debra Gould & Associates, LLC. Debra is an experienced workshop leader who specializes in self-development seminars in leadership, interpersonal, organizational, goal setting, and time-management skills. She delivers motivational and inspirational keynotes to corporations, professional associations, schools/universities and civic groups. Her personal and professional motto is *"Persistence Beats Resistance Every Time."*

Debra earned an M.S. Degree in Management from Florida Institute of Technology. She received her B.S. Degree in Accounting from Southern University at New Orleans. She is happily married to Joseph Gould, Jr. and the proud mother of Joseph Gould, III. Debra gives her audiences the tools to *Inspire, Motivate, and Grow!*

Contact Debra Washington Gould:

Debra Gould & Associates, LLC
P. O. Box 871211, New Orleans, Louisiana 70187-1211
Phone: (504) 244-6576
Toll Free: (800) 699-8091
Fax: (504) 243-2058
E-mail: djgould@gs.net
Website: http://www.tfrick.com/dga

Chapter 6

Determination, Desire and Destiny

STACY LYNN
SCHRIEVER

I recall being a young impressionable child sitting on the screened-in porch of my grandparents' house in Waco, Texas, listening to my grandpa's version of the facts of life. I believed that my grandpa was the wisest man in the world and that he could do no wrong, but what did I know? I was only eight years old. Although he had many professions in his life, the last one, as a high-school English and Latin teacher, is the man I knew him to be. I laugh when I remember that even though my brother and I lived in Texas, my grandpa would cringe when we would say "ain't" or "y'all," and God forbid we use the words "fixin' to"! (In translation that means "about to"). Nevertheless, he was a great storyteller, and I attribute my love of wise sayings and unique stories to his influence. I attribute my sense of humor, however, to his son, my father, who could always make any situation funny.

Donald Schriever, my grandpa, sat smoking a stogie and said to me on a starry night, "Always remember that there are two major characteristics in this world that set people apart from one another." As always, he would make me think about that statement before revealing the answer. Being a sponge for knowledge, I would eventually ask the obvious question, "Grandpa, what the heck are you talkin about?" He was stern when he said, "Determination and desire will make all the difference in the world." He followed this statement with words that will stay with me forever. He believed the most valued possession of a man is his word, and once it was broken, nothing could repair it. He also believed that everything in life is relative. When he said the word "relative," I was very confused until he explained it, and honestly, it was years later before I understood. "Relative" in the sense of wealth, health and knowledge relates to us all. No matter how poor one may be, someone is poorer, and no matter how much wealth one has, someone somewhere, is, of course, wealthier. The same is true for health: You may be sick, but someone is sicker. You may be smart or you can bet someone elsewhere is smarter — we all know people who are two bricks shy of a load.

I feel now, when looking back on what were very adult conversations with my grandpa, that he wanted to instill in me a sense of confidence. With determination and desire, plus the other advice that followed, maybe I would somehow find my way in life. Although many of our conversations were way over my head, I was blessed to have had them and felt a tremendous loss when he died of cancer. I was only twelve years old when he passed away, and I remember vividly the pain in my father's eyes when he had to tell me. I felt cheated because I didn't have a chance to say goodbye. Because I was sick with the chicken pox, I did not get to see him at Christmas, and it was soon after in January when he died. He gave me a lifetime of memories through his knowledge and storytelling, much of which I appreciate more now than I did as a child.

Years passed, and through ups and downs of a less-than-perfect childhood, I always remembered that determination and desire would be the keys to success. When I was about fourteen or fifteen, I overheard my dad talking to a coworker about me. I was nervous at first because I was afraid of what he might be saying about me to someone I did not even know. He was just chatting about his two kids when he suddenly said, " My daughter is unique; she is my surviving child. No matter how hard life hits her, she always manages to get back up and continue to fight; this quality of hers I admire." My dad admired me. What a great feeling I felt at that very moment. The impact that one conversation had on my self-fulfilling prophecy made me realize that life is full of obstacles and many uncomfortable changes, but our greatest glory is in never giving up — on life or ourselves. This belief has helped me survive endeavors in life when the odds were against me.

Ultimately, determination and desire will impact our destiny. The wisdom of my grandpa was useful, but I needed to define those words for my own benefit and development of character. Ironically, years later I found what I felt to be the best definition of determination and have used it ever since. When I experienced a great loss in a campaign for president of the Indiana Junior Chamber of Commerce, the next day my dad found a beautiful picture of a canyon with the sunrise just over the rocks showing a shadow of a runner in the scene. Below the runner the caption was simple but direct: *"Determination. The race is not always to the swift, but to those who keep on running."* I believe this caption defines my whole life sometimes. I guess he knew more than I did, because a year later I ran for president again and was not supposed to win, but I did. A year later, I still had desire, but determination was the key.

The road map of life can be full of potholes, barricades and bad weather, but a person's desire will determine if what he or she sees is an obstacle or an opportunity. I have often felt in dealing with salespeople that I would always take desire over talent any day because desire is coachable. It is heartbreaking to find people with enormous talent who lack desire, because desire, passion and motivation are just not teachable.

I have a cousin who had the perfect football physique growing up. He was, and still is, very stout and tall, like a linebacker, and he always looked older than his years. When he was eight years old, people thought he was twelve. My uncle believed he had found the ticket to retirement with this kid. My uncle had football hall of fame in his sights, but he was presented with a slight problem: My cousin's lack of desire. My cousin had the look, and as much as my uncle would push, his son would try, but he just wasn't into it. He lacked the competitive, killer instinct that drives a player to win. My cousin really did not enjoy or have the desire to hit another person full force or be hit himself. As much as my uncle wanted him to be successful, he could not give or teach desire.

January, 1998, Super Bowl with the Green Bay Packers and the Denver Broncos is an incredible example of talent versus desire. The prediction was Green Bay all the way because the line outweighed, could outplay and overall had better talent than the Denver Broncos. However, the secret weapon was the "want to" between the two teams. The pressure was off Denver and on Greenbay, so, with the leadership help of quarterback John Elway, the focus became desire. I will take desire over talent any day because it is heart and passion that keep success going.

Sitting in a movie theater with many others among millions who eventually saw the movie Forrest Gump, I realized how this character epitomized all that I speak about when I talk to associations about determination, desire and destiny. I loved the whole concept of this movie as it related to showing how one person can impact so many lives. Our determination and desire will affect other people and potentially their destinies. Forrest Gump was such a great example of all these qualities, as he saved Lieutentant Dan, who ultimately went on to be successful in the computer industry, got new legs, and fell in love. If not for the determination of Forrest in saving Dan's life, Dan would have had nothing. The extraordinary attempt at saving the life of Bubba also altered the destiny of Forrest with the promise of starting the shrimp business and fulfilling Bubba's dream. When Forrest asked his mother, played by actress Sally Field, "What's my destiny, Momma?" I thought they stole my momma's line. For years my mother had said to me that you have to do the best with what God has given you, and the journey will show your destiny — essentially the same advice that Forrest received.

She also would say that what you are is God's gift to you; what you become is your gift to God. This makes me think about how silly it seems when people ask children what they want to be when they grow up; just like Forrest would say when asked the question by Jenny while swinging their legs on an old oak tree, as a kid I would say, "I plan to be me when I grow up."

Life is like a book with many chapters, and you can't predict when one chapter will end and the other will begin. Destiny has a way of changing mid-flight in life somewhat unexpectedly. On December 6, 1997, I was living in Memphis, Tennessee, and my dad was visiting my friend Steve and me. During that day my dad wasn't feeling well; he looked like he had the flu. That night will remain unreal in my mind as if it had been a movie I had watched. It was not the flu, and the moments of that night seem to go in slow motion. As his eyes rolled back in his head and he slowly lost the ability to talk with any sense and began to have a type of convulsion, a panic swept over me. I yelled for Steve's help, grabbed a phone to call 911, and made a weak attempt to explain what I thought was happening to my dad. My mind was thinking that he was having a stroke or maybe going into diabetic shock. Within seconds he was white in color with no pulse, and he was not breathing. I was trained in CPR but my immediate reaction was panic. The 911 operator was talking to me as I was yelling at dad, and Steve looked me in the eyes, "Snap out of it! You know what to do. Do it now!" I threw the phone to Steve and proceeded to get my dad in a flat position, which was more difficult than it looked. Dad had been sitting up on a sunken leather couch when this began, so when he was flat on the couch I began to breath for him, which helped, but I needed the hard floor to perform proper CPR. Steve and I had to move a six-foot, 250-pound lifeless person to the floor, a load which should have been heavy, but at the time you just do what you have to do. Once I got him on the floor I began opening the airway, doing rescue breathing, and I just kept yelling at him to stay with me: "Please, dad, stay with me! He opened his eyes, but I could tell that he could not see me even though he was now breathing on his own. Steve went outside to help the paramedics find the house, and suddenly dad was gone again. I pounded and pounded on his chest with all the strength I had ever had in my life and deflated my lungs of every bit of air while still yelling out to him, "Please, dad, stay with me!" What seemed like a lifetime was probably just seconds, but suddenly he was back and breathing shallow on his own with a pulse that was faint but beating. The paramedics arrived, and a team of people took over. I watched in amazement eight to ten trained people save my dad's life. I recall thinking at that second how strange it felt to breathe life into someone who once gave me life.

Later, while watching the emergency room staff at the hospital, I realized how a team of people could change a person's destiny. When you call for a cardiologist in times of extreme urgency, you get not just one doctor; you get a well-acquainted team of people ready and prepared to save a life, with each person on the team acting with determination, having a look of the desire to help, and learning the ultimate gratification — the saving of a life. After the evening went on, the doctor asked me if I had any unresolved issues with my dad. He was blunt when he said that he wasn't sure dad would make it through the night. I took a deep breath, and without tears I explained that we had no unresolved issues, thank God, and although I was not ready for him to leave this earth for what I am sure was a far better place, if now was the time, I could handle it. The doctor had a most unusual look on his face as he walked back down the cold corridor of the ICU/CCU.

It was days later that I sat quietly in that hospital and realized that I was blessed, and the reason the doctor had had such an odd look on his face was that not many people could say what I said. So many people walk around with unresolved issues that continue to drain their energy every single day, and oftentimes the most minute problem drags on for years. What most people do not realize is if the person they have unresolved issues with dies, the issues, the feelings and the problem go unresolved. When I speak to people I ask them to fix all unresolved issues now before the moment passes them by and the worst feeling of all sets in — regret. Because of the events surrounding my dad, it forever changed my destiny with other people. When I shake people's hands, I look them longer in the eye and listen closer when they speak, and I more often tell people what and how I feel because we just don't know what tomorrow will bring.

Determination, desire and destiny can be considered life in 3D! I am convinced that any change or obstacle in our lives can benefit by the advice my grandpa delivered many years ago. If we face adversity with determination and look at leading our lives with the desire to steal every possible moment in order to make that moment great, our destiny should take care of itself. Like my mom and dad said, "We just rent space on God's creation and have to do the best with what God gave us, no matter what."

About Stacy Lynn Schriever

Stacy Lynn Schriever has ten years of sales and training experience. She performs keynote speeches and workshop/seminars as *"The Singing Speaker"* for all types of associations, businesses and organizations. Stacy owns "Keynotes In Song" and has provided such programs as, "Determination, Desire and Destiny," "Courage Heart and The Will To Win," and "America's Team, Are You in The Game?," are just a few of her inspirational talks.

Stacy is a member of The National Speakers Association and the American Society for Training and Development.

Contact Stacy Lynn Schriever:

Keynotes In Song
P.O. Box 2305, Arlington, Texas 76004-2305
Phone: (817) 469-9873
Toll Free: (888) 779-2219
E-mail: keynotes@flash.net

Chapter 7

Managing Change: An Inside Job

ABBY SHIELDS, M.ED.

> *"You must first be the change you want to see in the world."*
> MAHATMA GANDHI

As the Lord God was creating the world, He called upon His Archangels.

The Lord asked his archangels to help Him decide where to put the secret to being able to manage change.

"Bury it in the ground," one angel replied.

"Put it on the bottom of the sea," said another.

"Hide it in the mountains," another suggested.

The Lord replied, "If I do any of those, only a few will find the secret to managing change. It is so important

for humans to manage change. I have put change in the seasons, change in growing from an infant to an adult – oh, the list could go on and on!! Change is something everyone will experience in life. The secret to managing change MUST be accessible to EVERYONE!"
  One angel replied, "I know: Put it in each man's heart. No one will think to look there."
  "Yes," said the Lord, "Within each man's heart."
  And so it was....The secret to managing change lies within us all!

ANONYMOUS

Yes, the secret to managing change does live within us ALL. Unfortunately, when it comes to the subject of change, the memory bank of our mind associates the word *change* with negative experiences. Events such as divorce, hurricanes or job loss, bring great personal loss and pain, negative beliefs and fear. FEAR! We can't see it! We can't grab it and pack it away in a box, yet fear is ever-present when we hear the word *CHANGE*. Whether it is personal change, organizational change or educational change, the key to managing how you react to change is learning how to unlock the fears that keep you stuck in self-defeating behavior. In learning how to manage change from the "inside," I have found the following keys will help you unlock the doors of fear and self-limiting beliefs and take you along the path of significant progress in learning how to manage change.

Key # 1: Accept the fact that you cannot change what has already happened to you.

> *Forgetting those things which are behind ...*
> *I press toward the goal.*
> PHILIPPIANS **3:13-14**

So many individuals today live their lives focusing on past experiences and circumstances. In doing so, they live with statements like "If only"... or " I should have".... The sooner we realize that we cannot change what has happened to us in the past, the more energy we will have to focus on today. When teaching people how to overcome circumstances that they often times had no control over, I have them repeat the following line: "At some point and time in my life, I must give up all hope for a better yesterday." I do not remember where I learned that line (if anyone knows the original source of that quote, please let me know so I can give credit where credit is due). People laugh when they realize just how true that statement is. So many people sit around and hope for a better yesterday, wishing this didn't happen or that didn't happen. The sooner you realize and accept that you can't get yesterday back, and that in most cases we did not have control over what happened to us, the sooner you can begin to focus your energy doing today what needs to be done for a better tomorrow.

To be able to let go of the hurts and disappointments of the past, it is important to take a look at your belief systems.

Two steps you can follow to help you overcome your negative beliefs towards the change that might be taking place or that will take place are:

Step One: Identify your self-limiting beliefs: Please note that I did not say "other — people-limiting beliefs." I said SELF-limiting beliefs. In my trainings on managing change, one of the first things I do to help individuals overcome self-defeating behavior is to identify their belief systems that keep them stuck. Listed below are some of the more frequent beliefs that people have in regard to their ability to deal with the changes or events that might be taking place in their life:

- I must be perfect.
- Everything I do should go easily and without effort.
- It's safer to do nothing than to take a risk and fail.
- I should have no limitations.
- If it's not done right, it's not worth doing at all.
- I must avoid being challenged.
- If I succeed, someone will get hurt.
- If I do well this time, I must always do well.
- Following someone else's rules means I am giving in and I am not in control.
- I can't afford to let go of anything or anyone.
- If I expose my real self, people won't like me
- There is a right answer and I will wait until I find it.

- I'm not smart.
- I can't think right.
- No one understands me.
- I have no significance.
- My life has no meaning.
- Everyone is out to get me.
- I'll get even.
- No one appreciates me.
- I can't.
- I don't deserve this.
- I am not pretty enough.
- I'm too big.
- I'm too small.

The list could go on and on. Take a look at how many of these self-limiting beliefs you have and have come to understand. This determines your belief system through your circumstances and your ability to deal with the change taking place is what determines how you respond.

Please note *Diagram A.*

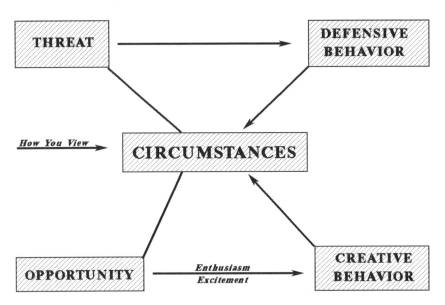

An excellent example of internal belief systems and their relationship to personal response to circumstances is the man we all think of when the country of India is mentioned. Our memory bank immediately brings forth the name Gandhi. Was it his "dressed for success" look that made him famous? I don't think so. How about his position in government? No. He did not have a position in government. It was his belief system. He truly modeled the natural law of "as within, so without."

So how do you begin to develop a positive belief system about change? View change as an opportunity. As mentioned earlier, most people view the effects of change as negative. To manage change from the inside, begin to focus on the positive outcomes of change. Personal growth and new opportunities are just two positive outcomes of change. What you focus on is exactly what you are going to see. Focusing on change as an opportunity can help change your paradigm, which in turn can help you embrace the limitless possibilities that face you as you are passing from the ending of what was to the beginning of what will be. A verse from the book *"Basic Instruction Before Leaving Earth"* that has helped me to do this very thing is *Philippians 4: 8 – 9*: "Finally brothers whatever is true whatever is noble whatever is right whatever is pure whatever is lovely whatever is admirable if anything is excellent or praiseworthy think about such things and the God of peace will be with you."

Step Two: Know that you are simply marvelous. I am amazed at the number of people I meet who do not live their lives with confidence and they cover up their feelings of inadequacy with masks. It is no wonder, then, when change of any type occurs, individuals are often in the dark as to what to do. To be able to rise above your circumstances, you must begin to realize that you are a marvelous creation, and you *do* have the ability to achieve excellence. Unfortunately, we often strive to be perfect. In trying to reach the level of perfection, our self-talk becomes filled with "if only's" and "I should haves." This oftentimes causes our thought processes to become filled with the self-limiting beliefs I addressed earlier. When we realize that we are marvelous creations that the same creator of great fishing holes or magnificent sunsets created us, we can be filled with the strength to face challenges that change often brings head-on. You ARE simply marvelous!

There is a story about a man whose memory was slowly fading, and upon examination the doctor said that an operation on his brain might stop any more memory loss. There was only one catch: The surgery was delicate, and there was a possibility that a nerve might be damaged and he would become totally blind. When asked what he would rather have, his sight or his memory, the man responded, "My sight, because I would rather be able to look where I am going than to remember where I have been." So it is with managing change: We do have a choice of whether we want to see where we are going or sit and focus on the past. I ask, which one would you choose if the doctor were to ask you the same question?

KEY #2 : Become Aware of Your Greatest Fear.

When change of any kind takes us out of our comfort zone, it is usually a given that at some point in time during the process of change an individual will be confronted by fear, which often leads to indecision, distress and adversity. When you begin to identify the fears behind your inability to cope with change, it is much easier to face the challenges that come with change.

The amazing thing about most fears is that they are illusions of our minds. They do not exist, but what power they have over our ability to manage change!

The following scenario is often what happens when we are confronted by our fears:

- Fears lead us to inaction.

- Inaction leads to no experience.

- No experience leads to ignorance
- Ignorance brings increased fear.

The cycle continues to repeat itself, thus bringing about self-defeating behavior. The key to overcoming your fears and managing change is *action*. When you change inaction to action, the cycle then looks something like this:

- Fear is faced with action.
- Action brings forth experience.
- Experience leads to wisdom.
- Wisdom brings decreased fear.
- Decreased fear brings increased success.

In helping to identify the fears that lead you to self-defeating behavior, take a look at your self-talk when it comes to facing daily life. If your self-talk is:

_____ I'll get inspired later;

_____ I better wait till I can do it right;

_____ If I wait long enough, I won't have to decide;

_____ I need more facts and figures before I can do anything;

_____ What if I finally do my best, but am still mediocre;

_____ If I decide, I might not get the chance to change my mind;

_____ There's a right answer and I'll wait until I find it;

_____ I should have no limitation;

_____ I might as well not start if I don't have time to finish;

_____ I need to make sure I follow the rules;

_____ I really should do what I am told;

_____ If it is not done right, it is not worth doing at all;

_____ I must be perfect;

_____ If I do well this time, I must always do well;

_____ It is safer to do nothing than to take a risk and fail;

It is quite possible that you have fallen into a performance trap. In other words, your self-worth is dependent upon your performance. This trap brings about fears, such as fear of failure; fear of success; fear of not being in control; and fear of what others might think. What might the effects of these fears have on an individual's behavior in dealing with change? These people become driven, perfectionist, depressed, or resentful. All of these behaviors give them a sense of being in control. As long as they are in control, they feel secure in who they are. One of my participants in my training once told me that his motto for living was "If at first you don't succeed, destroy all the evidence that shows you even tried!" When he hid the evidence that he had even tried he was making sure that he never looked like a failure.

If your self-talk sounds like:

_____ This is boring, I'll do it later;

_____ I never thought it would take this long;

_____ Rules are made to be broken;

_____ I'll do it, just leave me alone;

_____ If I am successful, I might become predictable;

_____ If I accept other people's routines I will lose my independence;

_____ Details! Details! Details!

_____ If I am successful, I might need to be responsible;

_____ I feel that I need to help everyone;

_____ I just can't say no;

_____ If I am successful, I might lose my friends;

_____ What if they don't like me;

_____ If I'm successful, I will hurt someone else;

_____ I don't know if I can;

_____ It's lonely at the top;

_____ I don't deserve success;

You probably are controlled by fear of rejection, or fear of being controlled by others. The fear of rejection often causes one to become an approval addict. Your sense of identity is caught up in having other people like you, because you might not like yourself.

The effects of these two fears in dealing with change cause people to become angry or depressed. By becoming "people-pleasers," they try to control the circumstances or other people to avoid being hurt.

No matter what change is taking place in your life, there is freedom in identifying your deepest fear. Marianne Williamson said it best in her course in miracles:

- Our deepest fear is not that we are inadequate…
- Our deepest fear is that we are powerful beyond measure;
- It is our light, not our darkness, that most frightens us.
- We ask ourselves, who am I to be brilliant, gorgeous, talented, fabulous?
- Actually, who are you NOT to be?
- You are a child of God. Your playing small does not serve the world.
- There is nothing enlightened about shrinking so that others will not feel insecure around you.
- We were born to make manifest the glory of God that is within us.
- It is not just in some of us;
- It is in everyone.
- As we let our own light shine, we unconsciously give other people permission to do the same.
- As we are liberated from our own fear,
- Our presence automatically liberates others.

Become liberated from your fears. Live from a position of strength; give your worry to God, and whatever you do, don't give up. You will come out of the tunnel of transition from the old to the new in one piece! **Enjoy** the journey!

KEY # 3: Seek the Invisible!

When unwanted change occurs, people try to seek the visible to help them cope with the changes that have taken place. Alcohol, drugs, overeating and shopping are just a few of the things people resort to for comfort during the time of change.

When our three-year-old foster daughter drowned in our backyard pool, I resorted to overeating, and 100 pounds later, I woke up and realized that I needed to seek the invisible instead of the visible. When unwanted change occurs, try to seek and lean on the following:

FAITH: I do not remember where I heard this definition of faith but I find such strength from it. "Faith is being sure of what we hope for and certain of what we cannot see." Faith is not a gift — it is a choice. We can either have faith that things will work out or choose to whine and complain about our circumstances. Faith, as it relates to change, can be best explained with the example of a man on the trapeze. As he is swinging in midair on his way to the opposite bar, he must have faith:

1. that the bar will be there;
2. that he can grab hold of the oncoming bar.

In order to grab hold of the new bar, he must first let go of the bar he was swinging on. So it is with people going through change. We must have faith to let go of what was and grab hold of the future. We grab hold the future by examining our strengths and coming up with an action plan that will move us in that direction.

In having our faith tested through trials that come with change, we should … "…consider it pure joy because the testing of your faith will develop perseverance." *James 1:2* Faith, just like my silver tea service, cannot stay bright unless it is polished daily and used. It is only when I come to seek the invisible and rely on my faith that I can continually polish my belief that all things will work together for good so that my faith shines through me to liberate not only myself, but others, from their fear of change. If you have faith, there is nothing to fear.

LOVE:

> *"If I have a faith that can move mountains but have not love, I am nothing. If I give all I possess to the poor and surrender my body to the flames, but have not love, I gain nothing."*
>
> 1 CORINTHIANS 13

When I mention the word LOVE, it is not the huggy, touchy-feely "stuff." When I mention love, it refers to what your behavior needs to reflect, no matter what change you go through. When you walk in love as you go through change, I encourage you to:

- Be patient, kind;
- Do not envy, boast or be proud;
- Do not be rude, self-seeking or easily angered;
- Do not delight in evil;
- Rejoice in the truth;
- Always protect, trust and hope;
- And Persevere!

When you walk in love as you go through change, you come to realize that you might not have had control over what has happened to you, but you do have control over how you respond to what happens to you. When you lean on love, you will respond to change in a positive way.

JOY:

> **"There is no '10' count in life. You are not out until you decide to stay down on the canvas."**
> **(Anonymous)**

How true that quote is! Helen Keller said that… "life can be a daring adventure or nothing at all." When you lean on joy to help you through unwanted change, you learn to give thanks for the blessings that you *do* have. So many of us let worry, blame and pity-parties get in the way of the pure joy of living. There are usually two types of people in my managing-change trainings. There is the individual who wakes up in the morning and says "Thank you, God, for this morning." or the individual who wakes up and says "Good God, it's morning!" When you lean on joy, you meet each day with a heart of gratitude, NO MATTER what the circumstances.

KEY # 4: Know why you woke up this morning.

When Alice in Wonderland came to the "fork in the road' and didn't know which way to go, she asked the Cheshire cat which way he thought she should go. The cat responded by asking Alice which way she wanted to go. When Alice said that it "didn't much matter," the cat stated, "Then it doesn't much matter which way you go."

Truer words could not be spoken. When you know why you wake up in the morning, you become grounded in your personal mission statement, and unwanted changes might set you back for a moment, but with your eyes focused on your purpose, you will be able to overcome any adversity that might get in the way. I have seen dramatic changes in individuals who take the time to develop a personal mission statement. The personal mission statement gives them a goal to focus on, even when the waves of life are rough. My personal mission statement is to inspire, encourage and promote the divine in all of us. That is why I speak. That is why I write. That is why I parent — and so forth. It becomes a reality check for my actions. If at the end of the day I see that my actions were not in alignment with what my personal mission statement is, I then take a look at where I can change behavior for the next day.

When you begin to manage change from the inside out, you will begin to feel a passion for living that you never had before. Max Lucado states in his book, *When God Whispers your Name,* changing direction in life is not tragic. Losing passion in life is. Something happens to us along the way... convictions to change the world downgrade to commitments to pay the bills. Rather than make a difference, we make a salary. Rather than look forward, we look back." It is an exciting feeling to have the passion for living return.

I do not make a claim that the four keys covered in this chapter are the only things you need to have to walk the pathway of change. What I do stand on is the fact that if you use these four keys to unlock the doors of managing change, change will not keep you knocked off your feet. You will rise above your circumstances.

About Abby Shields, M.Ed.

Abby Shields, M.Ed., is a dynamic international speaker and author who has the ability to bring objectivity, sensitivity, enthusiasm, and a liberal dose of humor to her programs. Shields has given numerous presentations across the United States and internationally on topics that focus on value-based communication, self sabotage, and interpersonal skills and most recently was asked to speak to the Social Security Department for the country of Belize on management skills.

Abby's clients say that she redefines the phrase, "global warming" with her quest to soften the edges of today's world as she lays down the cornerstone to her dream that all people will one day treat each other with dignity and respect.

Contact Abby Shields:

5060 Sharp Road, Mandeville, LA 70471
Phone: (504) 674-7872
E-mail: gabyabby@cmq.com

Chapter 8

Doug Smart, CSP

You Know Something They Don't Know About Change

"How many of you would say that in the last twelve months your professional life has gone through *significant change*?" I asked this question of the human resource department directors and staff of Chevron Chemical Company, gathered for their annual management retreat. They didn't hesitate a moment — all hands shot up. All, that is, except that of one middle-aged gentleman seated in a way that he was also leaning against the wall. I glanced at him, smiled, and nodded. Scanning the audience, I emphasized, "My hand's up, too! I've gone through significant change, too! Look around. There are people here from California to Hong Kong to Brazil. 97% of the hands are up. Look at the ship we are aboard — the *S.S. Significant Change*! Take a look around. All hands are up *but one.*" Feeling mischievous and not wanting to miss the opportunity to reinforce a salient point, I looked again at the wall leaner, paused, smiled (he smiled back), and wryly, coolly suggested, "That's all hands but one — and you, sir, are going to get fired!" He grinned and the room erupted into laughter. "You aren't keeping up with the pace of change in this organization." Facing the audience, I continued, "If you're not changing in a significant way — you're not growing in a significant way. Ray Kroc, the founder of McDonalds admonished, 'you're either green and growing, or ripe and rotting.' Either way, you are changing. There's no staying the same."

For the past few years, I've asked the question, "How many of you would say that in the last 12 months your professional life has gone through *significant change*?" to audiences as diverse as lumber mill supervisors for Georgia-Pacific, rocket scientists at N.A.S.A., regional managers for Mitsubishi Motor Sales, administrative staff at City of Hope Cancer Research Hospital, educators at the University of Illinois, financial managers for U.S. Customs Service, and lawyers at Rockwell International. Surprisingly, in every profession and industry, 90% or more of the audience members raise their hands. Like the rest of us, they live and make a living in an era of significant change.

We are all changing, but not everyone handles change equally well. Why? How do you learn to deal with change? How do you get people onboard the ship with you to quit grumbling and arguing that the ship needs to stay in familiar waters? This chapter will teach you answers that work.

Seeking Comfort

Besides a belly button, the ability to smile, two feet not four, plus a few more characteristics, there's something every one of us has automatically — a *comfort zone*. Our comfort zone is a registry of all of the experiences you or I has ever had. Its purpose is to supply wisdom gained from our experiences and instantaneously apply it to make snap decisions that protect us. For example, when you are in a performance review with your boss, it's your comfort zone that keeps you from jumping up, stretching your arms wide, and belting out a song. Another example: It's your comfort zone that prevents you from taking your shoes off as soon as you enter, and flinging them across the grocery store. In these settings, both behaviors are considered inappropriate. You have the abilities to burst into song and to toss your clothes around — and you do these things in the privacy of your home (at least, I do!), but in public, these activities are deemed *not right*. The comfort zone helped you "decide" to censure these impulses — at least until you are in an appropriate setting. Another example: Your mind is drifting as you leisurely drive your car, but out of the corner of your eye you catch a glimpse of sunlight flashing off of truck metal. Instinctively, your foot automatically springs off of the gas pedal and quickly mashes the brake pedal, because you know from past experience the glimmer of sunlight is moving too fast to stop at the intersection you are about to enter. A fresh, new driver won't have that "instinctive" ability and must turn his or her head to see the truck approaching, gape in horror, consciously remove the foot from the gas pedal, swing it over the brake pedal, push it down hard to stop the car, and pray that this multi-step maneuver was completed in time to avoid a catastrophe. In this case, your comfort zone acted as a decision making shortcut that saved you from harm — much like your automatic reflex system causes you to jerk your finger tips away from a hot casserole dish. It is estimated that 99.9% of all decision making flows through the comfort zone.

Change is the enemy of the comfort zone since it disrupts the automatic flow of decision making. Quite simply, change makes us uncomfortable. Change is like a fresh haircut — we usually feel better about it after we've had a couple of days to let it grow out and let it "grow on us", i.e., we get comfortable with the new way it looks. When it comes to how we deal with change, people fall into one of three categories: embracers, accepters, avoiders.

Embracers: It is estimated that about 20% of people enjoy change. We thrive on it. We actually find the adrenaline surge, produced when bracing for the unknown, invigorating. If an idea sounds good to us, we feel comfortable embracing it with little or no hesitation. For example, Barbara says, "Mike, I love your idea — you know, what you said in the meeting yesterday. I thought about it last night and it makes perfectly good sense to me. I don't know why we didn't do it your way years ago. I've got a couple of questions about procedure, but I'm with you on this one. Let's go!"

Accepters: 50% are willing but cautious when it comes to change. Ken says, "Mike, I like your idea — you know, what you said in the meeting yesterday. I guess it's a good one. It seems right. I don't know. There are other possibilities to think about. Can you send me something in writing? Let me think about it and I'll get back with you. Just send me something."

Avoiders: 30% of people instinctively dislike change. Their gut reaction is to slow down change, stop it, or worse,

"Let's go back to the [safe and comfortable] way we used to be." Since civilization in the 21st Century is zooming forward with unprecedented speed, would you guess these people are particularly comfortable with the pace of change in their industry? Are they comfortable with the pace of change in their own organization? I say they are particularly *un*comfortable. They are prone to feeling frustrated and stressed. This 30% causes approximately 80% of the friction in your workplace. You can generally spot someone in this mode by his or her instantaneous and defensive use of comfort zone-protecting phrases like: "We tried that before. You'll never get approval. It costs too much. If it isn't broken, don't fix it. The *right way* to do this is..."

To keep this useful generalization in perspective, it helps to bear in mind that on some issues an individual will be an embracer, on others an accepter, and on the rest, an avoider. None of us is a single-dimensional cartoon character. We adjust our approach to change according to how we feel about the circumstances. It helps to think of lava lamps — the colorful bubbles that rise and fall are us as we travel through the three levels. It is important to understand these feelings in ourselves — but what about when you want the people around you to accept your new idea for change?

Know that You Are S. M. A. R. T. about Change

Here's a given that works in your favor: 100% of people eventually change. They might not change when you want. They might not change the way you want, but, everyone changes. For example, look at the life cycle of our modern society: You are born, grow up, start a family, work really hard to provide for your family, grow old, and go live in a home until it's over! At what stage is there not constant and significant change? None! Life is change — yet 30% of the people around you (including coworkers, bosses, customers, friends and family) are putting their energy into disproving this fact in the name of comfort.

Let's talk business. Who is most valuable in your industry *now* —

1.) individuals who embrace positive change;

2.) those who are non-commitulant at first but usually eventually accept the improvements; or

3.) those whose gut reaction is to fight it? I'm voting for the first. I did some team training for Eaton Corporation at a computer switch manufacturing facility. A slogan on their training room wall succinctly said it all: "Our only competitive advantage is our people." Isn't the competitive advantage diminished by individuals who neglect to embrace opportunities that will help move the organization forward?

How can you be more comfortable as a person who embraces change? How can you win others over to accepting change you want to see implemented? Here is a **S. M. A. R. T.** approach.

Stay receptive to change. Sometimes this means a change in attitude is the first step. A gentleman in his 50's told me he eats the same thing for lunch every work day — hamburger and fries. Of course, I asked *why*, and he looked at me as if I was particularly dumb while he answered, "Because, that's what I like." I had to know if he ever broke the comfortable pattern. He said coworkers were always teasing and scheming to get him to eat new foods and occasionally he joined them for lunch. He tried new things but never enjoyed them because, as he said, "I don't go for all that strange food like chili or gumbo. And, besides, *I'm too old to change now*."

My mom used to call people like that "set in their ways." This may sound unkind, but I call them "set in their graves." You can't grow if you can't change. I know people who take comfort in dismissing conscious change in their lives because they think that weathered American proverb applies to them, "You can't teach an old dog new tricks." Sure, there is comfort in routine, but if the routine becomes out of synch with an environment that'll lead to happiness, the results can be perpetual discomfort. Let's face it, the business environment is always changing. Because of workplace restructuring, many people have jobs today that evolved around them — they wouldn't even apply for their current job if asked! This means flexibility and risk taking are valuable attitudes in today's workplaces.

Fortunately for Sam Walton and his family, he didn't try to stay comfortable as a small town variety store owner. At age 44, he bravely opened his first Wal-Mart and dreamt BIG. Mary Kay Ashe felt uncomfortable enough to challenge the safety of the *status quo*. She embarked on the scary adventure of starting her own cosmetics company at 45. Ray Kroc was a milk shake machine salesman of limited success when, at 54, he gambled on his first McDonalds. Eugenia Garside, of Cape Cod, Massachusetts, said, "It's kind of late but I'm glad to have it." when she received her high school diploma in 1998 at age 98!

All four of them knew that life won't improve by obsessing on how to keep things the comfortable way they've always been. And they also appreciated that "being too old to change" is faulty advice. Stay receptive to change through a healthy attitude toward positive change.

Make people comfortable with change (including yourself). Let's say you're at a meeting in your organization. You have a new idea you are excited about and you truly believe it will be an improvement. Your coworkers have never heard your idea before — you are the first to articulate it. What percent of people can you count on to oppose you? Figure 80% [computed by adding the accepters (50%) plus the resisters (30%)]. On the first hearing of a new idea, expect about 80% of the people in your meeting to resist your great new idea.

Is rejection a normal response to a good idea? Yes. Here's an example that hits close to home. Let's say you arrive home after work and your significant other says, "I had a really hard day. Let's go out to eat." You like the idea. Money is not an issue. You say, "Okay," and then ask, "Where do you want to go?" Significant says, "*It doesn't matter to me — wherever you want to go.*" Not wishing to play a game of back and forth, you say, "Okay, okay. Let's go eat at The Red Onion." As soon as Significant hears The Red Onion, he/she says, "No, I don't feel like eating there." (!) What happened? On the first hearing of a brand-new idea, approximately 80% of people will automatically oppose you — including the people who love you!

To put this in perspective: The comfort zone is an instantaneous decision making helper and it distrusts the unfamiliar. On the first hearing of a brand-new idea, the comfort zone feels threatened, and finds it is easier to repel your idea than to be vulnerable to discomfort by welcoming it.

The automatic tendency to resist is natural. Here's a quick test: if you were stranded on a desert island with plenty of food you brought with you, would you experiment eating the native berries and fruits that you didn't recognize? The odds are, your comfort zone would make you suspicious of them as possibly harmful. In a similar fashion, our minds stay on guard against ingesting potentially "harmful" ideas.

Obviously, idea filtering is beneficial, but what if you are too cautious? How to get around this resistance tendency in yourself? It helps to broaden the range of experiences registered in your comfort zone by trying new things to stay in the rhythm of change. How to get around this resistance tendency in others who may automatically oppose your great new idea? Here are some suggestions that the audience and I developed during a training session for Hawtal Whiting, an international automotive design firm:

- Fire the 80%. (Joking!)
- Prepare for the resistance.
- Politic and win over the 20% *before* your public announcement of your idea.
- Gain early support of several key people whose opinions are valued by others.
- Don't let the 30% get you down.
- Instead of asking for an immediate decision, just *plant the seed* of your idea.
- Educate them *now* — win them over *later*.
- Remember it's not what you say, but how you say it.
- Let them think it's their idea.
- Ignore instantaneous opposition ("We tried that before.")

- Soothe their comfort zones with a phrase such as, "If I can show you a better way..."
- Be persistent.
- Smile.

Ask for what you want. Winston Churchill said, "If you have an important point to make, don't try to be subtle or clever. Use a pile driver. Hit the point once. Then come back and hit it again. Then a third time — a tremendous whack." The comfort zone distrusts ambiguity and welcomes clarity. To help yourself become a stronger change embracer, be crystal clear with yourself about your goals and the results you want. To help other people make changes, be crystal clear about what you want them to do or think. The enhanced clarity will make it easier for them to deviate willingly from their natural pattern of behavior.

Here's an example of how a proprietor changed the behavior of potential customers. It was supper time in the food court at the mall and the crowd was thin. The choices were Oriental, Italian, Greek, a salad bar, Mexican, and a yogurt place. Behind the counter at the Flaming Wok, a middle-aged Oriental woman passionately took action to tilt the odds of success in her favor. In thickly accented English, she crowed at every potential customer within ten feet of her counter, "Hi! Want to try some?" as she held aloft a morsel of steaming spicy chicken skewered by a neon colored toothpick. If they looked at her she flashed a proud smile. About half pretended not to hear and deliberately looked away. Nearly all of the ones who looked accepted their reward, and about half of them bought something from her stand. At the other food shops the service people waited on customers, cleaned in anticipation of business, or leaned on the counter and watched the mall world float by. No one else offered samples nor asked potential customers to buy. In the 20 minutes I watched, her eatery garnered nearly as much business (including mine) as all of the others combined. The competition probably had good products, but she alone was willing to do what they would not — she *asked* potential customers to try her wares. She made herself clear — she wanted them to change their eating habits and to choose her food that night.

Reward and Re-enforce New Behavior — Yours and Theirs.

Arthur Schopenhauer, a German philosopher, observed a new idea goes through three stages in becoming "the norm":

- First, it is ridiculed.
- Second, it is violently opposed.
- Third, it is accepted as self-evident.

Not everyone deals equally well with change. I managed a real estate office and was always looking for ways to improve our service and gain a competitive advantage. Our phones didn't stop ringing when we closed the office at 5:30. I decided that we should stay open an hour later on weekdays so that customers could contact us after they got home from work. Some of my agents (about 20%) thought this was sensible. The rest, basically, hit the roof. They wasted no time informing me, "It's a waste of time. This idea has been tried before with marginal success. The calls will be administrative, not new business. Other companies don't do it." Also, there was considerable concern that it would negatively impact their personal time. The grumbling faded away in about four weeks. Two months later there was no opposition at all. About then, the competitors started staying open later. The reward for adjusting the behavior? We experienced several things: a few more sales that might have been lost because we were unavailable, more commission dollars for the agents, increased visibility in the community, and thanks from several customers for having sensible hours that accommodated working people. To ease the discomfort of the change, I stayed later — as a symbolic gesture — and I lavished thanks and praise on my salespeople for backing our effort to become the real estate company of choice for customers in our community.

The theme of Dr. Michael LeBeouf's book, *The Greatest Management Principle in the World*, is a good one to remember as it will serve you well: Behavior that gets rewarded gets repeated.

Try New Things and Stay in the Rhythm of Change.

A lake that doesn't receive fresh water becomes stagnant. To keep my mind bathed in "fresh water," I like to try 50 new things a month, which is about two on most days. I don't keep count, but when I have choices to make, I am conscious about the possibility of choosing something different just for the sake of different. My wife, daughter, and I all play a little game when one of us is grocery shopping. We buy an item we have never bought before simply because it is new to us. We spend less than two percent a month extra on our food bill (and our pantry is full of inedible food!), but it transforms an ordinary task into a little adventure of finding new ways to surprise less than two percent a month extra on our food bill (and our pantry is full of inedible food!), but it transforms an ordinary task into a little adventure of finding new ways to surprise everyone at home. More importantly, for sound psychological health, in a small way it reminds us to refuse to be imprisoned by the rut of the mundane.

I commend to you to try 50 new things a month, and to keep them simple. Some easy things you can do this week are: Put on a tie or jewelry you enjoy but hardly ever wear because it's "too good for every day." Take the long way home and look for attractive architecture you never noticed. Make a phone call or write a letter you have dreaded. If you are a loner, volunteer. If you are gregarious, let someone else tell the last joke. Compliment a cashier. Read a book for guilty pleasure. Give an anonymous gift. Make a decision that makes you face one of your fears, especially if it makes you feel uncomfortable. In short, go out of your way to do simple things that you don't routinely do.

Be sure to try new things in your relationships, too. Relationships can also become trapped in the rut of the mundane. In a presentation I did a couple of years ago, I suggested this same idea of trying 50 new things a month. I'll never forget, at the break, a young man (I guess about age 25) approached me with a handshake and an enthusiastic smile as he gushed, "Thank you!" His mood was contagious. I looked up at him and couldn't resist smiling broadly as I said. "You're welcome! Thanks for what?"

"You just gave me my wife's birthday present!" he said.

"Birthday present? What do you mean, birthday present?" I replied.

"Let me explain. Tomorrow is her birthday. We have been married for four years. We don't have a lot of money and I love her so much. I really wanted this to be *the* special birthday. I didn't know what I was going to do — until you said, 'Try 50 new things a month, about two a day.' That gave me an idea!"

I thought, "I bet it did tiger. I bet it did."

"Tomorrow, when she opens her card, I'll have written in it, 'I love you so much that every day for the next 30 days, I'm going to dream up a fresh new way to tell you just how much I love you.'"

Isn't that a sweet thought? I bet lots of people would find that gift priceless. My mind immediately went to, "Hey, you're getting off cheap!"

My wife has heard me tell this story in keynotes, but somehow it didn't occur to me to follow my own advice — that is, until last Valentine's Day. I bought a big red card and wrote in it, "I love you so much that every day for the next 30 days I'm going to dream up a fresh new way to tell you just how much I love you." She silently read it and started to cry. I thought, "Yes! I made am impact!" For the first few days it was fun. Then it became work! I would wake up in the morning in a mild panic and think, "What am I going to do today?" Curiously, I noticed my gift evolved into the little things that say "I love you." I complained less, held hands more, did some cooking, and I cleaned up after the dog — without even being asked!

Try new things to stay in the rhythm of change. Be sure to include changes that keep your important relationships fresh.

Today Forward

In the past twelve months, significant change has probably impacted both your personal and professional lives. The comfort zone, not being a fan of change, may have put you, and the people around you, on the defensive and blocked receptivity to changes that are healthy. How to be more receptive to positive change? You now know something they don't know: on any new idea you can expect 20% to embrace it, 50% to take a non-committed position that may later change to acceptance, and 30% to have a "knee-jerk" opposition and instinctively try to avoid the change. When approached with a new idea, people fall into one of three categories: embracers, accepters, and avoiders. To be more willing to accept change personally, it helps to understand your feelings. Ask yourself, "Which one of the three am I in when it comes to___(the change)___?" When you want others to more willingly trust your judgement and accept change, ask yourself, "Which one of the three is _(name)_ when it comes to___(the change)___?" This will help you formulate approaches that succeed more often because you are more attuned to your comfort zone and that of the people whose lives you impact.

Be **S. M. A. R. T.** about change to help guide you through hyper-changing times:

- **S**tay receptive to change.
- **M**ake people comfortable with change (including yourself).
- **A**sk for what you want.
- **R**eward and re-enforce new behavior — yours and theirs.
- **T**ry new things and stay in the rhythm of change.

Enjoy the fun and feelings of greater success as you embrace positive change.

About Doug Smart, CSP

Call Doug Smart, CSP, to get participants laughing, learning, and leading. Doug is an author, radio personality, keynoter, and trainer who has spoken at over 1,000 conventions, conferences, seminars, sales kickoffs, and management retreats. He works with leaders who want to make this their best year yet! Doug's *"Smart Ideas Series"* boosts resiliency, productivity, leadership, and creativity. His diverse client list includes AT&T, Columbia HCA, IBM, Mitsubishi Motor Sales, Southern Methodist University, Kansas State Government, and U.S. Department of Education.

Doug is the author/co-author of: *TimeSmart: How Real People Really Get Things Done at Work, TimeSmart: How Real People Really Get Things Done at Home, Reach for the Stars, FUNdamentals of Outstanding Dental Teams,* and *Sizzling Customer Service.*

Contact Doug Smart, CSP

Doug Smart Seminars
P.O. Box 768024, Roswell, GA 30076
Phone: (770) 587-9784
Fax: (770) 587-1050
E-mail: DougSmart.Seminars@att.net

Please E-mail Doug's office to request a free subscription to "SMART IDEAS for Leaders" E-Newsletter.

Chapter 9

JEAN HOUSTON SHORE

When the Handwriting is On the Wall: What to Do When It's Time to Change

I had not tasted fear this bitterly in a long, long time. I was going to have to make a decision — and right now. Before me rose an eight-foot wall of solid rock, covered with a few hewn-out footholds and a very flimsy looking piece of rope. Behind me stood the other members of our trail-riding expedition, and they all would miss the spectacular waterfall view ahead if I couldn't make myself conquer this steep rock face. My thoughts raced — "I signed up for horseback riding, not rock climbing! I hate heights! What if I slip and break all of my teeth out? All these people are counting on me! Jean, you can do this! NO, YOU CAN'T!"

Finally I looked around the group, I met each person's eyes, I took a deep breath and I scaled that rock wall! Once I was at the top I started shaking like a leaf. But I also wanted to cry for joy because I knew that I had just won an internal battle – the battle of change reluctance.

Only rarely does our need for personal change confront us as clearly as the wall of stone confronted me that day. In fact, sometimes we don't even perceive our need for personal change. Unfortunately, those around us often perceive our need for change all too clearly. For example, how many of us have watched a family member or a colleague slowly lose control of his or her life through abuse of drugs, alcohol or food? Of course, we see that person's circumstances from the outside while the person actually lives in the *middle* of those circumstances. No matter how hard we try we can't convince another person to change until he or she accepts that there is a need for change.

Most of us who have lived a few decades can point back to times when we needed to change, but we didn't recognize the "handwriting on the wall." Perhaps we have been trapped in a dead-end job or in an industry whose viability has become questionable. Maybe a relationship has gone sour and something needed to be done — but we were the last ones to pick up on that fact.

In this chapter, we will look at three facets of personal change and how they interrelate. First, I'll discuss three attitudes that can keep us from seeing the handwriting on the wall. In this section we'll also examine how adults and children view the boundaries of change differently. Next, several examples will show how we can recognize our need for personal change. Finally, I'll present nine steps you can follow to successfully make personal changes in your life.

Missing the *time-to-change clues* in life causes us to be less productive, less successful and ultimately less content with life. A starting point in becoming more efficient in personal change is examining our own feelings about change. How do we feel about change in general? I've found that there are generally three common problematic attitudes.

Three Problematic Attitudes

The "I Can't" Short-Sell
Some of us openly admit our change reluctance, selling ourselves short in the process. I remember a few years ago when I developed a chronic problem with my right shoulder. Since sleeping on my right side seemed to aggravate the problem, my husband and I decided to switch sides of the bed. When I mentioned this casually to my parents, my mother was incredulous. "I could never change sides of the bed with your father," she said. "We're just too set in our ways."

I still smile when I think of that exchange because I am firmly convinced that mom was selling herself short. Of course she could learn to sleep on the other side of the bed! What she said was "I can't." What she meant was some combination of "I don't want to," "I don't' see why I should," and "This change will be difficult for me."

Many of us do the same thing. We see an obstacle in front of us that we think will require more of us than we had planned to give. So we take what we think is the easy way out. We sit back, pout, and give everyone who will listen our adult version of "I can't."

To be more successful we should instead focus on the I CANs of managing change. Below are eight key skills anyone can practice to master change reluctance. When you feel your self-doubt start to rise in the face of change, respond with one of the following affirming statements, or make up one of your own!

I CAN RECOGNIZE FEAR IN OTHERS:

Our colleagues or family members also face times of change and their reactions can affect ours. Discovering the motivations underlying the behaviors of others can help us in choosing to respond most appropriately.

I CAN AVOID OVERREACTING:

Often, we overreact to change when we feel fear ourselves. When people feel fear, they react to change emotionally, not logically. Knowing that our behaviors can become fear-based allows us to guard our behaviors so that we don't make our situations worse.

I CAN ASSESS THE CHANGE WITH OBJECTIVITY:

Many kinds of changes happen in the course of a lifetime. Moving from one neighborhood to another can seem devastating to a child, but in hindsight, the change doesn't seem so bad after all. Just as parents counsel their children to see the bright parts of moving (new school, new friends, a bigger room), we also must learn to evaluate all parts of a change rather than focusing only on that part that seems the most difficult. There are good sides and bad sides to every change; we simply must train ourselves to see them.

I CAN FORM MY OWN OPINIONS:

It sometimes seems that our creativity goes out the window when we are faced with opportunities for personal change! We hear about an impending change, and almost immediately the company "buzz" becomes loud and clear. It is easy to see the situation using only the dimension of popular opinion; it is much harder to start from a clean slate and form our own opinions based on the facts.

I CAN LET GO OF OLD PATTERNS OF BEHAVIOR:

Managing change reluctance means forcing ourselves out of our "comfort zones." Often even patterns of behavior that have served us well must be replaced with new habits to take us into the future. As difficult as it is to abandon our old comfortable "shoes," sometimes a new, better-designed pair will serve us more suitably, even if the new shoes take a while to break in.

I CAN LEARN NEW SKILLS:

Learning anything new takes some effort. Often when we say that we can't do something, we really mean that we do not want to put forth the effort needed to learn *how* to do it. Until our minds start to fail, we can learn new skills if we put forth the right amount of effort and have the right level of training.

I CAN ASK OTHERS FOR HELP:

Mastering personal change is rarely done alone. We need the feedback and support of others to truly begin to demonstrate the needed changes. To get others to help us, we must first be willing to admit that we cannot do it all by ourselves.

I CAN ENHANCE MY SENSE OF SELF-WORTH:

A healthy sense of self-esteem is at the center of any successful change. While working on change in a particular area of life, we should do things to bolster our self-esteem in other areas. For example, perhaps you are trying to use a new management style and the change is difficult for you. Keep a balanced sense of self-worth by finding gratification in the things you are already good at doing. Celebrate the strengths you already have, even as you are working to build new strengths. If too much emphasis is placed on the area you are trying to change, you run the risk of becoming hyper-focused and you will be unreasonably disappointed if you fail to reach the goal you have established.

The "Of Course I Can" Lie

Others have a different problem with change reluctance. As I work with my business clients, I hear many of them profess to be good at dealing with the changes in their industry. Then, in the next sentence, they'll say something like, "I can't wait until things get back to normal around here!" This comment does not earn a high score on any change aptitude scale! This is, in my view, *change-denial* and we all face it at one time or another. Change-denial happens when we feel overwhelmed by the level of change required. We are so reluctant to even consider our need for personal change that we can't see how reluctant we are!

Another cause of change-denial behaviors is the underestimation of the change required. Often, we see changes in the work environment as opportunities for us to make minor "tweaks" while others complete radical overhauls. If a person's attitude toward change is really change-denial, he or she will probably begin to see his or her need for change once the combination of time passing, work situations being handled poorly, and telling comments from others begin to shine a light on the self-deception.

The "I Don't Need to Change" Values Conflict

Then there are those among us whose behaviors would indicate that there is no need for them to change in any way. For example, a participant in one of my recent sessions was loud, brash and rude to almost everyone in the room. My guess is that everyone who meets this person would say he could benefit from a change in certain group interaction behaviors! But so far he sees no need to change — because he makes lots of money. Apparently, his personal value system says that abusing his co-workers is an acceptable strategy as long as the sales keep pouring in! Do you think that this person has really thought about how his behaviors make him appear? I find it hard to believe that this man does not want to be considered a "kind and decent human being." I prefer to believe that this person simply has a level of confusion between his internal values system and his behaviors.

Each of us has a system of internal, core values. Some people have worked through their systems of values. They are sure of what they believe and the priority of each component of the system. Most people are not so sure. When faced with a decision that needs to be made (such as the question of if one should consider changing his or her behaviors), these people do not know how to choose consistently. With time and a structured process of values clarification, the gentleman in my class would probably conclude that not only does he want to make lots of money, he also wants to be perceived as a "kind and decent human being." Then, with his values conflict settled, his interpersonal behaviors would begin to change.

Change and the Playpen

Sometimes small children react better to change than adults do. Take, for example, a toddler in a playpen. The little one is bounded in on five sides: in front, in back, on the left, on the right, and below. For a while the young child will be content in the playpen, distracted by the toys we allow into his or her world. The playpen provides a place of supervision and safety as the child develops both physically and mentally. Child development experts tell us that a child's natural development of physical vision will be less than optimal if he or she is left in the playpen too long. To develop good vision, a child needs to focus both close up (as in the playpen) and far away (as while strolling in a city park.) Children must know this somehow because they certainly become displeased with the playpen world quickly! Developing, healthy children want out! They don't feel the need to be confined by the artificial boundaries of the playpen.

Somewhere along the line, though, many adults decide that the boundaries of our adult worlds (job, family, money, work hours, community involvement, residence) suit us just fine. Sure, we may complain about our self-imposed limits from time to time, but just let an outside force attempt to take us out of our playpen-world! We scream bloody murder! "Put me back in! Put me back in!"

Our reasons for screaming vary. We may prefer the inside of the playpen because it is familiar and comfortable. Perhaps we're secretly afraid that the big world outside our current life-boundaries will be less fulfilling, less exciting, and less meaningful. Maybe we would prefer to stay inside our playpens because we are not sure we'll be successful outside of them. Whatever the reason, adults tend to dislike any situation that takes them past the territory they have already conquered. Our boundaries help us frame reality and so, to be safe, we tend to not look beyond them. But sometimes situations force us outside our playpen-worlds, whether we choose to go or not.

The Alarm Clock: Recognizing the Need for Change

Not long ago I sat on a crowded airplane as we prepared for takeoff. Comfortably leaning back on the airline's tiny pillow, I was beginning to doze when I was rudely awakened by the irritating sound of beep-beep-beep, over and over. "One of those alarm watches or a pager or something," I thought. Other passengers began to look around and shake their heads too as the noise continued and continued. No one made any move to stop the noise. I looked at my watch — no, it wasn't me. I settled back and waited for someone to fix the problem. A few moments later, after everyone on the plane had begun to complain about the problem, the flight attendant began to walk the aisles trying to find the beeping source. Finally, she stopped close to my seat and retrieved a black bag from the overhead bin. "The noise seems to be coming from in here," she said. "Whose bag is this?" I glanced up and with horror recognized my computer bag. Suddenly the beep-beep-beep of my bedside alarm sounded very familiar! As the whole plane watched, I sheepishly opened the bag and shut off the alarm clock I had hurriedly tucked inside. How embarrassing it was to have to admit that *I* was the one who needed to change, especially after I had joined in the other passenger's complaints!

It seems to be much the same way in many of our personal change situations. We simply don't recognize our need for change until one of three things happens. First, we recognize our need for change *after a crisis.* Our job is eliminated and we quickly recognize our need for a change in job direction. We have health problems (a heart attack perhaps), and suddenly the idea of watching our cholesterol makes sense. A family member is hurt in an auto accident, and we are jolted into reexamining how we've been prioritizing our time. This sort of change is reactive, but it results in personal improvement nonetheless.

Second, we can recognize our need for change *after having accomplished a goal*. Usually, this sort of "change-clue" comes to our attention more slowly. After the euphoria of having accomplished something has faded, we begin to feel a bit ill at ease. We find that we need to set a new, higher goal and, if the goal is lofty enough, we'll see that we cannot accomplish this new goal with our current set of skills. This sort of change is proactive and goal-driven, and it results in steady, planned bursts of personal improvements. The challenge is that this approach may result in goal setting and improvements in only a few areas of focus. It's also possible that we may continue to set and achieve goals that do not matter in the "New World" environment.

Third, we can recognize our need for personal change *after intense self-examination*. We are a very busy society, running to and from work, soccer games, community activities and social events. Very few of us take time each year for personal "strategic planning." If we would conduct personal "management retreats" and systematically examine our strengths, weaknesses, opportunities and threats as successful organizations do, we would surely find opportunities for personal improvement! We could analyze which of our interpersonal skills and habits worked well in the last year and which did not produce the results we wanted. Then we could draft action plans for improvement and build in accountability with people in our lives. This sort of change catalyst is probably the most effective one of all. When we recognize our need for change through regular self-examination, we are being proactive, logical and progressive in our approach to personal improvement.

Nine Steps to Making Personal Change

Once you have recognized a need for personal change, the steps to mastering it are fairly straightforward.

First, **REST ON YOUR FOUNDATIONAL VALUES SYSTEM**. We know that our behaviors must be aligned with a well-defined sense of personal values. When you know you need to change, take some quiet time to reexamine your personal system of values, to recommit to those things that are most important in your life. This provides you with perspective and a sense of stability while you are undergoing the transition period of this change.

Second, **IDENTIFY THE ENVIRONMENTAL CHANGES** that are causing you to need to change. Has increasing competition in your industry resulted in a corporate reorganization? Find out all you can about WHY this is happening. Your research will give you answers to some of your questions; it will also enable you to avoid the change-denial problem many of us face when we are overwhelmed with the magnitude of change.

Third, if you need to, **GRIEVE FOR THE PAST**. Do what you must to gain closure before you move on into the "New World." Pretending that your move from the old way-of-being into the new way-of-being will be easy is just another form of change-denial. Celebrate the successes of the past and then wipe the slate clean in order to start the future with strength and resolve.

Fourth, **PROJECT THE BOUNDARIES** of how you will be required to change. Give some fact-based, logical thought to how what will be required of you in the "New World" is *similar to* and *different from* what was required of you in the "Old World." Chances are, at least some of your boundaries haven't changed all that much. For example, while a forced move from the Sales Force to Account Management would change the boundaries of your compensation, colleagues, and travel schedule, the boundaries of the corporate culture, product lines, and industry served would probably remain close to the same. Looking at boundaries in this way will allow you to see the change more objectively rather than overreacting in fear.

Fifth, after you have projected your boundaries logically, **DOUBLE THAT PROJECTION TO GET YOURSELF MENTALLY READY.** This step takes you out of your "comfort" zone and into your "creative zone." You probably have a good grasp of what the personal change will require of you. Now take a step back and think about the wild and crazy things this change could cause. This move into Account Management could put you in touch with a new customer who would like your professionalism, and he or she could offer you a job managing West Coast Operations. Then you could move to California and learn to surf!

Sixth, **IDENTIFY AND RECRUIT YOUR SUPPORT TEAM.** None of us wants to feel alone when we're pushing the limits of personal change. We need to have those around us who will encourage us, challenge us and hold us accountable for progress. The best members of your support team would be those who have experienced periods of personal change themselves. A person with an "I'm perfect just the way I am" attitude doesn't generally make a very pleasant or effective supporter. Speak with the members of your support team and ask them to "coach" you through this period of adjustment. Clearly communicate your expectations to each member of your support team: Are they to act as passive sounding boards, active opinion-givers or somewhere in between?

Seventh, during this period of personal change you may need to **NEGOTIATE SOME TEMPORARY BREATHING ROOM.** Who you'll need to negotiate with depends on what sort of breathing room you need. For example, if your personal change involves taking a class at your local college, you may need breathing room in the form of assistance with transporting the kids to and from soccer practice. A neighbor, a parent, a spouse, or a sibling might be able to help. Remember that the breathing room arrangement is temporary, just until you get into the swing of your "New World.'

Eighth, solidify your change commitment by taking time **TO WRITE AN "I COMMIT TO CHANGE" ESSAY**. The essay doesn't have to be long or grammatically perfect; it simply has to capture the facts and feelings that surround your situation. When the essay meets with your approval, share it individually with your support team members. Help them to see how important making this change is to you. Ask them to be diligent in their support. Post your essay where you can review it periodically.

Finally, the ninth step is simply to **BEGIN.** Every change in behavior has a starting point. You can choose whether to begin right away or whether to delay your personal change effort. The challenge is to become fully aware and to make sure that your behaviors are always aligned with your system of personal values.

A Moment in Time Commitment

Here is an illustration of a day when I "saw the handwriting on the wall." I was in the Women's Center waiting area. I think I was reading about Tony Bennett. The article was somewhat interesting, but it shouldn't have commanded my full attention. Still, I half-read, half-mused about life and waited for part one of the dreaded annual mammogram. In my experience, it's a two-step process: Step one is having the film taken; step two is finding out what the radiologist saw on the film. I remember that the 50ish woman to my left sat rigidly still. I didn't look at her, preferring instead the doctor's-office ritual of feigning interest in the latest People magazine.

A few moments later, the technician called the woman's name, and she went in for step two of the process. The examination room was only a few steps away from me, and the door didn't close completely. A moment later I watched the technician speak two very important words to the woman: "It's clear." In a split second, the woman was a flood of emotion. She burst into tears and gushed, "Oh thank you! Thank You! I don't have cancer after all? Are you sure? Oh, thank God!"

In my waiting room chair, I cried too. I understood — finally. The woman beside me had been afraid for her life, sent to the lab because a doctor had found a suspicious something. While I was reading an article about Tony Bennett, she was wondering if she was going to die.

I am a person who professes to care deeply about other people, even those I don't know. Yet in that moment I really blew it. I missed my chance to be a source of comfort to another soul who definitely needed a warm touch. If only I had looked her in the eye, offered a friendly smile, even held her hand in mine as she waited for the news! I could have helped a hurting person even if only for a moment in time. I deeply regretted my single-minded preoccupation with self. And I resolved that I'd do better next time.

My experience taught me that opportunities for personal change come when you least expect them. Through properly identifying our attitudes toward change we master our change reluctance and increase our change aptitude. By learning to recognize our need for personal change we save time, set more workable goals and even achieve more life balance. Finally, through following the Nine Steps to Making Personal Change, we mobilize our resources to achieve the change we desire.

This sums up the stuff of personal change: circumstances with a human connection that shine a light on our personal need for change followed by a resolve to respond more nobly in the future. As we continue our adventures beyond familiar limits, let us seize each moment to make a difference in our worlds.

About Jean Houston Shore

    Jean Houston Shore helps executives, managers and employees improve their lives by improving themselves. She owns the Business Resource Group, a seminar company assisting both businesses and associations. Jean's programs help her audiences align vision and values, producing practical results. She is best known for her educational and inspirational presentations including *Leadership With Vision, Making Great Things Happen,* and *Personal Bannering.* Jean's consulting clients repeatedly say that she possesses an uncanny ability to uncover core business issues and ask the tough questions needed to get them back on track.

    Jean's life experience includes broad business knowledge through her early work as a Certified Public Accountant, multicultural exposure through her teaching of Total Quality Management principles in the U.S., Canada and the United Kingdom, and a real-world entrepreneurial view as the owner of a small business. Jean has worked with a diverse base of clients including people from AT&T, CIBA Vision Corporation, New Mexico 4-H, Indiana CPA Society, The Academy of Medical-Surgical Nurses and many hospitals and professional associations.

Contact Jean Houston Shore:

Business Resource Group
408 Vivian Way, Woodstock, GA 30188
Phone: (770) 924-4436
Fax: (770) 924-1128
E-mail: shorebrg@mindspring.com

Resources for Change

Bob Googe

WOW Performance Coaching, Inc.
10680 Loire Ave., San Diego, CA 92131
Toll Free: (888) WOW-YOU-2
E-mail: wowseminar@aol.com

Debra Washington Gould

Debra Gould & Associates, LLC
P. O. Box 871211, New Orleans, Louisiana 70187-1211
Phone: (504) 244-6576
Toll Free: (800) 699-8091
Fax: (504) 243-2058
E-mail: djgould@gs.net
Website: http://www.tfrick.com/dga

Mike Monahan

Performance Coach
1153 Bergen Parkway, Suite M-181, Evergreen, CO 80439
Voice and Fax: (303) 674-3186
Voicemail: (800) 759-2881
E-mail: M2HRA@aol.com

Nick Nicholas, CSP

ProMax and Associates, Inc.
3999 Austell Road, Suite 303-362, Austell, GA 30106
Phone: (770) 439-8900
Toll Free: (800) 925-5788
Fax: (770) 439-8909
E-mail: nicknicholas@writeme.com

Stacy Lynn Schriever

Keynotes In Song
P.O. Box 2305, Arlington, Texas 76004-2305
Phone: (817) 469-9873
Toll Free: (888) 779-2219
E-mail: keynotes@flash.net

Abby Shields

5060 Sharp Road, Mandeville, LA 70471
Phone: (504) 674-7872
E-mail: gabyabby@cmq.com

Jean Houston Shore

Business Resource Group
408 Vivian Way, Woodstock, GA 30188
Phone: (770) 924-4436
Fax: (770) 924-1128
E-mail: shorebrg@mindspring.com

Doug Smart, CSP

Doug Smart Seminars
P.O. Box 768024, Roswell, GA 30076
Phone: (770) 587-9784
Fax: (770) 587-1050
E-mail: DougSmart.Seminars@att.net

Bruce Wilkinson, CSP

Workplace Consultants, Inc.
1799 Stumpf Blvd., Bldg. 3, Suite 6B, Gretna, LA 70056
Phone: (504) 368-2994
Fax: (504) 368-0993
E-mail: SpeakPoint@aol.com

Index

Keeper Notes

Keeper Notes